PERFORMANCE
APPRAISALS
MADE
EASY

This book is dedicated to our supportive husbands, Mike and John, and our ever patient canine companions, Ollie and Sam!

LISABETH S. MARGULUS
JACQUELYN ANN MELIN

PERFORMANCE APPRAISALS MADE EASY

Tools for Evaluating
Teachers and Support Staff

CORWIN PRESS
A Sage Publications Company
Thousand Oaks, California

For information:

Corwin Press, Inc.
A Sage Publications Company
2455 Teller Road
Thousand Oaks, California 91320
www.corwinpress.com

Sage Publications Ltd.
1 Oliver's Yard
55 City Road
London EC1Y 1SP
United Kingdom

Sage Publications India Pvt. Ltd.
B-42, Panchsheel Enclave
Post Box 4109
New Delhi 110 017 India

Printed in the United States of America

Library of Congress Cataloging-in-Publication Data

Margulus, Lisabeth S.
Performance appraisals made easy: Tools for evaluating teachers and support staff / Lisabeth S. Margulus and Jacquelyn Ann Melin.
        p. cm.
Includes bibliographical references.
ISBN 0-7619-8894-7 (cloth : alk. paper)
ISBN 0-7619-8895-5 (pbk. : alk. paper)
1. Teachers—Rating of—United States. 2. School employees—Rating of—United States.
3. Teachers—Job descriptions—United States. 4. School employees—Job descriptions—United States. I. Melin, Jacquelyn Ann. II. Title.
LB2838.M3765 2005
371.14′4—dc22   2004012025

This book is printed on acid-free paper.

04   05   06   07   7   6   5   4   3   2   1

Acquisitions Editor:	Robert D. Clouse
Managing Editor:	Elizabeth Brenkus
Editorial Assistant:	Candice Ling
Production Editor:	Denise Santoyo
Typesetter:	C&M Digitals (P) Ltd.
Cover Designer:	Anthony Paular

Contents

Acknowledgments

Corwin Press gratefully acknowledges the contributions of the following individuals:

Albert Armer
Principal, Wortham Elementary School
Wortham, TX

Royce Avery
Principal, Woodsboro High School
Woodsboro, TX

Glen Clark
Principal, American Fork High School
American Fork, UT

Robin Dexter
Assistant Professor
College of Education, University of Wyoming
Laramie, WY

Robert McCarthy
Assistant Professor
College of Education, University of Wyoming
Laramie, WY

Phil Silsby
Principal, Belleville West High School
Belleville, IL

Patti Vickery
Principal, Woodsboro Junior High School
Woodsboro, TX

About the Authors

Lisabeth S. Margulus has worked as a teacher and administrator at all grade levels of traditional and alternative K-12 schools. Her experience has included high-need, urban settings as well as suburban and rural schools. Her area of specialty has been leadership training. This has included districtwide consulting and, during a 3-year sabbatical from education, directing a strategically linked, outcomes-based professional development program at a healthcare center employing 2,800 people. She has also worked extensively in the business and manufacturing arenas in the area of workplace performance.

Margulus frequently consults in the areas of Leadership Development, Workforce Performance and Accountability, and Parent Involvement and Accountability. Her approach always begins with an analysis of skills and a review of the client's job description. She then reviews the skills analysis and identifies the "gaps" between what is desired and what is current behavior and performance. Finally, she meets with the employee and his or her supervisor to provide a plan of development to enable the individual to become successful. A complete "buy-in" from both parties is strongly recommended for maximum growth.

In 1999 she joined the Educational Leadership Department of the School of Education at Grand Valley State University in Grand Rapids, MI, where she is now Coordinator of the department. Margulus earned her Masters Degree in Staff Administration and her doctorate in Educational Leadership from Western Michigan University in Kalamazoo, MI.

Jacquelyn Ann Melin is Affiliate Professor at Grand Valley State University, where she teaches classes in curriculum development and differentiated instruction. She also serves as the Director of the School of Education Student Information and Services Center. She was a public school educator in Rockford, Michigan for 32 1/2 years, serving as an elementary- and middle-school teacher, as teacher/coordinator of gifted and talented students, and as an elementary principal.

Melin presents professional development seminars at the local, state, and national levels. She worked for Susan Kovalik and Associates for 6 years and did Model Teaching Weeks in Integrated Thematic Instruction. She also works for Staff Development for Educators and presents on science and mathematics instruction, character education, and differentiation. She has published *Passport to Learn* (2001), a book on meeting the needs of gifted learners in the classroom.

Chapter One

Introduction to the Performance Appraisal Process

WHAT IS A PERFORMANCE APPRAISAL AND WHY IS IT IMPORTANT?

Simply put, it is the observation and evaluation of a school employee's work behavior and accomplishments for the purpose of making decisions about the staff member. These decisions may include wage, salary, and benefit determinations; promotion, demotion, transfer, or termination actions; and coaching and counseling, training, or career development options.

There are three basic functions of an effective performance appraisal:

1. To provide adequate feedback to staff members on their performance

2. To serve as an opportunity to communicate face-to-face modifications or changes to existing performance objectives

3. To provide data to administrators so they can evaluate a staff member and judge future job assignments and compensation

The notion of performance appraisal has become an almost universally accepted fact of life in most organizations. It often serves as the basis for other human resource systems, such as salary management, career development, and selection processes. Because of all of these uses for the performance appraisal process, it is increasingly important that school leaders more than ever need to improve their managerial and supervisory skills in such areas as creating individual performance standards, getting employee commitment to performance standards, and conducting interim and end-of-year performance appraisal meetings.

This book was written to help school leaders not only improve their ability in managing their employees' performance, but also to provide staff members with coaching tools that will target their performance deficits. As the first step in any performance review process is to identify the knowledge, skills, and abilities that are required in a specific position, this book provides administrators with unique job descriptions for most support staff and teaching positions. This is not only beneficial for the administrator, but it is enormously important to the employee, as specific performance outcomes are outlined and presented. *Clear, stated behaviors and outcomes for workplace performance must be outlined and discussed if the administrator and the support staff member or teacher can possibly have success in this process. Both parties must have the same mental picture of their performance expectations.*

Self-appraisal forms are also presented for the job-specific responsibilities, as well as self-appraisal forms for more general, interpersonal skill areas that affect how employees interact with colleagues, students, parents, administrators, and others.

After comparing the staff member's expected performance with his or her actual performance, the school administrator can select relevant coaching tools from the book that the staff member can immediately use to help "close the performance gap." These coaching tools provide background information on each performance area, individual development plan forms, and a suggested reading list. The information presented in each area is not designed to be over-whelming, but rather to be practical and ready to use by an employee who needs help in closing a performance gap.

The book also provides school leaders with clear directions on how to conduct initial, interim, and formative coaching and summative performance appraisal meetings, as well as presents templates that immediately provide the employee with beneficial feedback and direction for improvement.

Why Is It Necessary to Have a Standardized Process of Implementing Performance Appraisals Throughout an Organization?

It is necessary to have a standardized process of implementing performance appraisals because it ensures that each individual is judged fairly and keeps dis-crimination out of promotions and compensation decisions. It also avoids legal challenges that could result from termination or promotion.

Moreover, having a standardized process ensures that job performance expectations are consistent throughout the school district. If employees are transferred from one building to another, they will be more comfortable with what is expected of them. This consistency will also improve staff morale, and this is a key benefit. It is well documented in many motivational studies that people perform better when they are comfortable and enjoy their work. They are able to focus all of their time and energy on the task at hand and not on potential fears or imagined crises. *Remember, teachers teach students skills and competencies and impart knowledge that will be measured on a multitude of tests. Support staff has responsibilities that support the teaching and learning process. If everyone is doing his or her job well, then student learning will be impacted positively.*

What Is the Process That Enables Change Most Effectively?

Several coaching meetings should be held throughout the entire performance appraisal process. Each meeting should be proactive and should build on each previous discussion and observation.

During each meeting, the administrator should:

- Put the staff member at ease if he or she is nervous. Engage in general conversation until the signs of nervousness subside.
- Review the agenda.
- Emphasize that the purpose of the meeting is to help the staff member work up to his or her potential and to challenge him- or herself.
- Use specific examples when discussing the staff member's behavior and performance.
- Help the staff member outline his or her individual development plan by using the performance appraisal coaching tools.
  - Set short- and long-range goals with the employee.
  - Select strategies and timelines for each goal's implementation.
  - Allocate resources if necessary.
- Emphasize your support for continued improvement and growth.
- Check the staff member's understanding; ask for a summary of key points.
- Make sure the staff member understands performance requirements for the coming period.
- End the meeting positively.

The purpose of this book is to provide busy school leaders with tools to develop teachers' and support staffs' competencies to ultimately enhance student achievement. These tools are not of uniform length and/or format, as the skills sets they address vary greatly. The tools will most effectively be implemented by using the processes listed in the box below:

Overview of the Performance Appraisal Process

1. Review the teacher or support staff member's job description and the summative tool to which he or she will be held accountable.

2. Ask the teacher or support staff member to assess him- or herself on each of the required competencies.

3. Observe the teacher or support staff member's performance (more than one visit—scheduled and unscheduled).

4. Meet with the teacher or support staff member to discuss what was observed and identify gaps in performance.

(Continued)

(Continued)

5. Give the teacher or support staff member any of the coaching tools from this book that will address his or her performance needs.
   - Explain the coaching tool thoroughly.
   - Demonstrate how the coaching tool should be completed.
   - Specify the date by which the coaching tool should be completed.

6. Discuss the completed coaching tool with the teacher or support staff member.

7. Schedule other observations to see how the teacher or support staff member has responded to the coaching.

8. Complete the summative performance appraisal tool.

9. Schedule the summative performance appraisal conference.

10. Get the employee's feedback on the effectiveness of the performance appraisal meeting.

Remember, the supervisor's primary concerns should be:

- The "what's" and the "when's," not the "how's." The staff member should be the steward of the "how's" in order to maintain his or her sense of control and creativity.
- To grow his or her staff members in order to develop the school's pool of skilled professionals for the future.
- To make training the result of an earnest skill gap analysis or part of the staff member's development and measured performance.

To summarize, the key principles behind the developmental performance appraisal system are:

1. Clear expectations are the backbone of the process.

2. Expectations must be agreed upon by the parties involved.

3. Keep the system as simple as possible.

4. The staff member and the administrator are accountable to one another.

5. They are both also accountable to their internal and external customers.

6. Expectations must have checkpoints throughout the process and must be written on the basis of observable and measurable behaviors.

7. Valid and reliable assessments are a major segment of the process.

8. Staff members are assets to be developed. Continuous learning and growth is a must for every staff member in the organization.

9. All school employees have a vital role in the success of the organization.

10. Development and training must be continually supported to be successful.

Chapter Two

How to Write Effective Job Descriptions

The Performance Appraisal Process begins with a thorough review of employees' job descriptions. The first drafts of job descriptions are usually furnished to the administrators by the human resource department (if available) after it has completed a thorough job analysis and completed all job specifications. The administrators then review them, adding any information that they believe is necessary to be included in the job description and job specifications. Finally, the administrator then meets with the employees currently in the jobs to make certain that all key responsibilities and competencies are delineated accurately. This discussion is valuable, as employees who perform the job are most capable of providing the details of their jobs most accurately. When employees are represented by a union, it is essential for the union representatives to be involved in the entire review process.

This inclusion, furthermore, will reduce the possibility of future conflicts. Enabling employees to make corrections, ask for clarification, and discuss their job duties with their supervisor greatly benefits staff or administrator communication and facilitates the staff's feeling of empowerment. Finally, as effective communication is a foundation for the establishment of a trusting relationship among all members of a school community, this important step must never be omitted from the performance appraisal process.

Once the job descriptions and specifications have been finalized and reviewed by all appropriate individuals, a system should be developed for ensuring that the job descriptions and specifications remain current. The Human Resources Department usually assumes this responsibility. This is a very important step in the process, as schools are dynamic organizations and responsibilities may change frequently. Rarely does a job remain the same year after year.

By using this overall process, employees and supervisors have summarized all job analysis information in a readable manner and have provided the basis for defensible job-related actions. They have also served all employees by providing documentation from management that identifies their jobs.

In designing job descriptions, there are major components which must be addressed:

- **Identification:** Lists the job title, reporting relationships, department, and location of position.
- **General Summary:** In 30 words or less, describes the purpose of the job. It will include the product or service required, the relationship of this job to others in the organization, and the impact of this position on other units in the organization.
- **Job Specifications:** Provides the qualifications needed to perform the job satisfactorily.
  - Knowledge, Skills, and Abilities (KSAs)
  - Education and Experience
  - Licensing (if required)
  - Specific Interpersonal Skills
  - Specific Technical Skills
  - Physical Requirements and Working Conditions. This information gives the information necessary to determine what accommodations might and might not be possible under the ADA (Americans With Disabilities Act) regulations.
- **Essential Functions and Duties:** Describes in clear and concise statements the major and secondary tasks, duties, and responsibilities to be performed by the employee in the position, how frequently these duties are performed, the level of decision making required, and the level of authority of the position.
- **Disclaimers and Approvals:** Enables employers to change employees' duties or requests employees to perform duties not listed, so that the job description is not viewed as a "contract" between the employer and the employee. A sample disclaimer may be:

  Note: The statements herein are intended to describe the general nature and level of work being performed by employees assigned to this position. They are not intended to be construed as an exhaustive list of all possibilities, duties, and skills of personnel so classified.

In summary, writing clear expectations for every position in the organization will translate job duties and responsibilities into performance targets that can be measured objectively. This process will prevent frustration and increase personal satisfaction on the parts of both the employer and the employee.

On the following pages, you will find examples of clearly written, current job descriptions for most employees in a school environment.

Support Staff

Job Description: Bus Driver

Name: _____

Dept/School: _____

Date: _____

JOB GOALS:

1) To safely operate the vehicle he or she is driving
2) To understand student behavior, including issues related to students with disabilities
3) To encourage the orderly conduct of students on the bus and to handle incidents of misconduct appropriately
4) To know and understand relevant laws of the road and local school bus safety policies
5) To handle emergency situations effectively
6) To safely load and unload students to their designated "home" locations

DESIRABLE TRAITS, SKILLS, AND ATTITUDES:

- Has a positive attitude toward the job, the students, and the staff
- Respects the values of confidentiality and integrity
- Has the ability to work independently, organize, and use time effectively
- Shows initiative, but is also willing to take direction
- Conducts oneself in a professional and ethical manner
- Works cooperatively with others, and has the ability to establish and maintain effective working relationships with other employees and the public
- Dresses appropriately for a school setting
- Is certified through a local or national Emergency Medical Response Training Program. (Desired but not mandatory)

REPORTS TO:

The School Bus Driver will report to the Director of Transportation in a large school district and to the Superintendent of Schools in a small district. The reporting structure can be revised appropriately dependent on size and circumstances of each individual school organization.

PERFORMANCE RESPONSIBILITIES:

- Complete a pre-trip inspection prior to each use of the bus
- Ensure that the bus is properly warmed up before the start of the trip
- Obey all traffic laws
- Observe all FCC regulations for the use of the two-way radio
- Inform the supervisor in ample time if unable to make a scheduled bus run
- Supervise the boarding and de-boarding of students
- Maintain discipline when students are on the buses
- Keep assigned bus clean each day
- Follow assigned routes and schedules
- Discharge students only at authorized stops
- Transport only authorized students
- Report all delays/accidents and complete appropriate forms
- Must complete a map/form showing routes, pick-up times, stops, and student names for each run assigned by the end of September each year, and shall update it on an as-needed basis
- Maintain at least one half tank of fuel at all times
- Attend meetings as requested or required
- Complete all required paperwork in a timely manner
- Follow all procedures, policies, and directives of the district
- Hold three fire evacuation drills during the school year
- Submit to regular physicals
- Perform other duties as assigned or needed

Support Staff

Job Description: Bus Driver (form continued)

Name: _____

Dept/School: _____

Date: _____

EVIDENCE OF PERFORMANCE:

- Attendance record
- Record of pick-up and delivery
- Citations and fines
- Routine inspections
- Record of arrivals
- Referral records
- Accident record
- Record of meetings with building staff
- Physical records
- Participation in specific training or workshop opportunities
- Demonstrates excellent interpersonal, time, conflict, and stress management skills

TERMS OF EMPLOYMENT:

School year with an annual evaluation. Wages and benefits as outlined in the contract.

Support Staff

Job Description: Counselor

Name: _____

Dept/School: _____

Date: _____

JOB GOALS:

1) To implement the Guidance Curriculum Component through the use of effective instructional skills and the careful planning of structured group sessions for all students
2) To implement the Individual Planning Component by guiding individuals and groups of students and their parents through the development of educational and career plans
3) To implement the Responsive Services Component through the effective use of individual and small group counseling, consultation, and referral skills
4) To implement the System Support Component through effective guidance program management and support for other educational programs
5) To use professional communication and interaction with the school community
6) To fulfill all other professional responsibilities

DESIRABLE TRAITS AND ATTITUDES:

- Has a positive attitude toward the job, the students, and the staff
- Respects the values of confidentiality and integrity
- Has the ability to work independently, organize, and use time effectively
- Shows initiative but is also willing to take direction
- Conducts oneself in a professional and ethical manner
- Dresses appropriately for a school setting

REPORTS TO:

The School Counselor will be responsible to the school administration.

PERFORMANCE RESPONSIBILITIES:

- Teaches guidance units effectively
- Engages staff involvement to ensure the effective implementation of the guidance curriculum
- Helps students, in collaboration with parents, establish goals and develop and use planning skills
- Demonstrates accurate and appropriate interpretation of assessment data and the presentation of relevant, unbiased information
- Counsels individual students and small groups of students with identified needs and concerns
- Consults effectively with parents, teachers, administrators, and other school personnel
- Provides a comprehensive and balanced guidance program in collaboration with school staff
- Provides support for other school programs
- Demonstrates positive interpersonal relations with students
- Demonstrates positive interpersonal relations with educational and support staff
- Demonstrates positive interpersonal relations with parents and community
- Shows a commitment to ongoing professional growth
- Possesses professional and responsible work habits
- Follows the profession's ethical and legal standards and guidelines

EVIDENCE OF PERFORMANCE:

- Performed specialized activities related to the school guidance program involving students, teachers, administrators, other staff, parents, and community agencies
- Provided crisis intervention assistance to school and students regarding emergencies when needed
- Documented individual and group counseling; student appraisal; consultation with school personnel, parents, and community agencies; coordination with other programs; and program evaluation and planning

TERMS OF EMPLOYMENT:

Hours as assigned by the principal. Pay rates and benefits as determined by the Human Resources Department. Initial probationary period required.

Support Staff

Job Description: Custodian

Name: _____

Dept/School: _____

Date: _____

JOB GOALS:

To provide a safe, clean environment for learning, which necessitates providing a link between jobs that are done in the environment every day to help ensure students' ability to learn and thrive

DESIRABLE TRAITS, ABILITIES, AND ATTITUDES:

- Has positive attitude toward job and clientele
- Conducts him- or herself in a professional and ethical manner
- Respects the values of confidentiality and integrity
- Has the ability to work independently, organize, and use time effectively
- Has the ability to work with frequent interruptions and adapt to changing circumstances
- Shows initiative, but is also willing to take and follow direction
- Works within the procedures and systems in the school community
- Dresses appropriately for a school setting
- Provides strong leadership to custodial staff (Good organizational skills, delegation skills, motivational skills)
- Works cooperatively with others and has the ability to establish and maintain effective working relationships with other employees and the public
- Must possess knowledge of occupational safety and health regulations
- Must have a solid knowledge of the utilization and care of materials and equipment used in the performance of his or her responsibilities
- Should be able to lift 50 pounds
- Be able to operate all cleaning equipment
- Be able to use basic tools for maintenance such as ladders, tools, etc.
- Be able to safely work with cleaning chemicals and refuse

REPORTS TO:

The Head School Custodian reports to the Building Administrator and to the Director of Operations.

PERFORMANCE RESPONSIBILITIES:

- Give timely attention to work orders
- Comply with all regulatory mandates
- Provide inservice to staff as needed
- Address all staff concerns
- Responsible for overall condition of building and grounds
- Assignment of duties to other custodians
- Approve overtime and keep record of overtime
- Order and maintain building supplies and maintenance of supply budget
- Dusts, sweeps, mops, scrubs, and vacuums hallways, classrooms, locker rooms, gymnasiums, cafeterias, large group rooms, and office space
- Cleans windows
- Empties trash and paper recycle containers
- Cleans restrooms and restocks soap, paper, and sanitary products
- Maintains building, performing minor and routine maintenance activities
- Notifies the Director of Operations (or other direct supervisor) concerning the need for major repairs or additions to lighting, heating, and ventilating equipment
- Cleans snow and debris from walkways
- General maintenance of grounds, including mowing the lawn and trimming the shrubbery
- Additional job duties may be specified in individual buildings

Support Staff

Job Description: Custodian (form continued)

Name: _____

Dept/School: _____

Date: _____

EVIDENCE OF PERFORMANCE:

- Number of complaints
- Specific observations
- Evaluation and supervision records
- Grievances
- File copies and complaints
- Participation in specific training or workshop opportunities
- Demonstrates excellent interpersonal, time, conflict, and stress management skills

TERMS OF EMPLOYMENT:

School year with an annual evaluation. Wages and benefits as outlined in the contract.

Job Description: Food Service Worker

Support Staff

Name: _____

Dept/School: _____

Date: _____

JOB GOALS:

To provide students with a nutritional food service program that will enhance their learning and behavior. Assumes responsibility for preparing and serving attractive, quality foods in an atmosphere of efficiency, cleanliness, cooperation, and friendliness and in a manner that maintains food safety and sanitation requirements.

DESIRABLE TRAITS, ABILITIES, AND ATTITUDES:

- Has positive attitude toward job and clientele
- Has the ability to work independently, organize, and use time effectively
- Has the ability to work with frequent interruptions and adapt to changing circumstances
- Shows initiative, but is also willing to take and follow direction
- Works cooperatively with others and has the ability to establish and maintain effective working relationships with other employees and the public
- Must possess the local county's Health Department Safety and Sanitation certification
- Must possess a high school degree or equivalent (GED)
- Must possess knowledge of occupational safety and health regulations
- Must have a solid knowledge of the utilization and care of materials and equipment used in the performance of his or her responsibilities
- Be able to lift 40 pounds
- Be able to operate all kitchen and technological equipment

REPORTS TO:

The Food Service Worker reports to the Food Service Manager or to the Director of Operations in a small district.

PERFORMANCE RESPONSIBILITIES:

- Food Preparation Duties
  - Completes assigned breakfast and lunch food preparation in designated work areas
  - Operates food service equipment in a safe and efficient manner
  - Maintains a clean and orderly workstation
  - Maintains records of foods prepared, used, left over, and discarded and records the information on the appropriate forms
  - Follows standards of food safety in preparing and storing foods. Dates new items received and rotates existing stock to ensure that it is used first
  - Assists in conducting food, supply, and equipment inventories
  - Cleans and sanitizes work areas and equipment
- Meal Service Duties
  - Arranges and organizes assigned service area per approved diagrams and procedures
  - Serves correct portions of food in specified dishes using standardized portion utensils
  - Monitors self-service areas and replenishes food and supplies as required
  - Practices good customer relations behaviors (speaking, smiling, and being solicitous and responsive to both students and staff)
  - Reports student discipline problems to the appropriate school staff member
  - Cleans and sanitizes assigned service areas before, during, and after meal service
- Point-of-Sale Duties
  - Operates point-of-sale cash register or computer terminal per standardized procedures
  - Completes point-of-sale daily reports at end of meal service

EVIDENCE OF PERFORMANCE:

- Record of food and supply inventory
- Complaints and official violations
- Observations and complaints
- Demonstrates excellent interpersonal, time, conflict, and stress management skills

TERMS OF EMPLOYMENT:

School year with an annual evaluation. Wages and benefits as outlined in the contract.

Support Staff

Job Description: Media Specialist

Name: _____

Dept/School: _____

Date: _____

JOB GOAL:

The media specialist is responsible for the general operation of the media center to maximize its use as a learning resource facility to support teaching and enhance student learning.

QUALIFICATIONS:

a. Possess a college degree in library science from an accredited institution
b. Have excellent interpersonal and collaborative skills as well as outstanding oral and written communication skills

DESIRABLE TRAITS AND ATTITUDES:

- Has a positive attitude toward the job, the students, and the staff
- Respects the values of confidentiality and integrity
- Has the ability to work independently, organize, and use time effectively
- Shows initiative but is also willing to take direction
- Conducts oneself in a professional and ethical manner

REPORTS TO:

The Media Specialist will be directly responsible to the School Principal.

PERFORMANCE RESPONSIBILITIES:

- Assist teachers in orienting students in the use of the library materials
- Help students to develop research skills
- Work with staff in a supportive role to develop a school program that effectively integrates the media center and classroom activities
- Assist in the development of skills related to technology
- Provide service to staff and students, assisting them in the selection of materials suited to their needs and abilities
- Promote reading, listening, and viewing of resource materials with staff and students
- Allocate the library budget
- Inform staff and students regarding new and existing materials
- Create and maintain an attractive, welcoming center
- Maintain the media center in excellent order with all resources ready for use by students and staff
- Supervise circulation of all materials
- Monitor the schedule for media center bookings
- Do minor repairs to damaged materials
- Prepare bibliographies, letters, and other media center documents
- Assist teachers in selecting, deselecting, and weeding media center materials
- Maintain all files and the inventory of all materials and equipment
- Coordinate use of A.V. equipment
- Attend professional development activities to improve weaker skill areas

NOTE : Some lifting and carrying of materials may be required.

EVIDENCE OF PERFORMANCE:

- Prepared and managed annual budget for print and nonprint materials
- Process new books, periodicals, and nonprint materials for shelves and entered bibliographic data into catalog
- Made resources available to students and teachers
- Developed flexible circulation, loan, and use policies
- Selected and ordered materials appropriate for grade level and curriculum of building
- Arranged scheduling of facilities and collections to meet the needs of individuals, small groups, and large groups for research, browsing, recreational reading, and viewing

TERMS OF EMPLOYMENT:

Hours as assigned by the principal pay rates and benefits as determined by the human resources department. Initial probationary period required.

Job Description: School Nurse

Support Staff

Name: _____

Dept/School: _____

Date: _____

JOB GOALS:

1) To implement a comprehensive program of health services for the school
2) To provide health services to students
3) To promote health education and preventative health practices for students

DESIRABLE TRAITS, SKILLS, AND ATTITUDES:

- Is a graduate of an accredited professional nursing education program
- Possesses a valid state nursing license
- Two years nursing experience, preferably in community health, pediatric, or family health
- Certified by the state to conduct vision and hearing screening
- Knowledge of health appraisal to identify student health defects
- Must maintain certification in CPR, vision and hearing screening, and as a health screener
- Has positive attitude toward job and clientele
- Conducts him- or herself in a professional and ethical manner
- Respects the values of confidentiality and integrity
- Has the ability to work independently, organize, and use time effectively
- Has the ability to work with frequent interruptions and adapt to changing circumstances
- Shows initiative, but is also willing to take and follow direction
- Works within the procedures and systems in the school community
- Dresses appropriately for a school setting
- Works cooperatively with others and has the ability to establish and maintain effective working relationships with other employees and the public

REPORTS TO:

The School Nurse will report to the Health Services Coordinator/Principal.

PERFORMANCE RESPONSIBILITIES:

- Provide temporary and emergency care for sick and injured students or staff according to district policy and procedures
- Be a health advocate for students
- Notify parents of accidents or illness and secure medical care for students in emergency cases (if parents or emergency contacts cannot be reached)
- Coordinate management system to administer medications according to district policy and procedures
- Perform health screenings as required by state's Department of Health
- Develop and implement continuing evaluation of school health program, and make changes based on findings
- Maintain confidentiality of all health information and records
- Provide health education to individuals and to groups
- Serve as health liaison between school, physicians, parents, and community
- Assess student problems and make appropriate referrals as needed
- Participate in a variety of school committees (i.e., School Improvement Team; Crisis Management Committee)
- Participate in assessment and reporting of suspected child abuse
- Make home visits to help with student health problems as necessary with the permission of the principal
- Communicate regularly with the principal (and health services coordinator if there is one) regarding health services issues
- Assist the Health Services Coordinator or Principal in developing and enforcing procedures for the administration, safety, and security of medications, first aid, or health supplies and equipment
- Review and evaluate immunization records
- Compile, maintain, and file all physical and computerized reports, records, and all other documents required, including clinic records and accurate, updated health records on all students

Support Staff

Job Description: School Nurse
(form continued)

Name: _____

Dept/School: _____

Date: _____

- Requisition supplies and equipment needed to maintain clinic inventory
- Report potential health and safety hazards to the principal
- Strictly comply with all district and individual school routines and regulations

EVIDENCE OF PERFORMANCE:

- Drug administration record
- IEP team record
- Observation and anecdotal record
- Complaints and documented records
- Conference and calendar records
- Conference record and staff response
- Timely submission of reports
- Documented reports
- Participation in graduate classes, workshops, or other specific training opportunities
- Demonstrates excellent interpersonal, time, conflict, and stress management skills

TERMS OF EMPLOYMENT:

School year with an annual evaluation. Wages and benefits as outlined in the contract.

Support Staff

Job Description: Paraprofessional

Name: _____

Dept/School: _____

Date: _____

JOB GOAL:

Assist teachers in the implementation of educational and therapy programs that address physical, mental, health, and safety needs of students.

QUALIFICATIONS:

a. Minimum Training and Experience: Must possess excellent oral and written communications skills (Note: Fluency in a second language or knowledge of distance learning may be required)
b. Desired Training and Experience: Two years of college and/or specialized training or experience related to assignment

DESIRABLE TRAITS AND ATTITUDES:

- Has positive attitude toward job and clientele
- Conducts him-or/herself in a professional and ethical manner
- Respects the values of confidentiality and integrity
- Has the ability to work independently, organize, and use time effectively
- Has the ability to work with frequent interruptions and adapt to changing circumstances
- Shows initiative, but is also willing to take and follow direction
- Works within the procedures and systems in the school community
- Dresses appropriately for a school setting
- Works cooperatively with others

REPORTS TO:

The teacher aide will work as an assistant to, and under the supervision of, a certified teacher(s) who retains the responsibility for the planning, instruction, supervision, and evaluation of the students. The Teacher Aide is responsible to the principal through the teacher.

PERFORMANCE RESPONSIBILITIES:

Working under direct supervision of one or more teachers, a Teacher Aide may be required to perform some of the following tasks:

- Adapt classroom activities to the capabilities of the student. Encourage the student to function as a member of the group by involving other students in activities and encouraging independence and self-help skills
- Implement individual program
- Assist the teacher in providing data for student evaluation
- Alert the teacher to any special circumstances regarding the student
- Assist with large or small groups or individual students
- Comply with and assist in teacher's methods of maintaining classroom discipline
- Assist with field trips
- Monitor the students in class and on the playground to prevent danger and to reinforce social and learning behaviors. May participate in travel, training, and off-campus activities
- Receive the students from the bus, parents' cars, etc.; ensure that students are picked up after school
- Conduct prescribed therapeutic and exercise programs for physically exceptional students
- Attend to personal needs of disabled students in the program, i.e., feeding, toileting, general care to maintain comfort. Secure students in walkers or other equipment, move or position students, etc.
- Participate in all facets of the program designed to develop the language, independence, mobility, and self-help skills of severely disabled students, under the direction of a licensed teacher or multidisciplinary team

Support Staff

Job Description: Paraprofessional
(form continued)

Name: _____

Dept/School: _____

Date: _____

- Assist in maintaining individual student's progress records for review and program planning. Provide observations on progress, behaviors as required, and work as a member of a multidisciplinary team as required
- Prepare instructional material under the teacher's direction
- Clean and store materials and equipment after use
- Display students' work and prepare bulletin boards displays
- Mark objective lists and routine exercises
- Continue to improve expertise and job-related skills
- Perform other responsibilities as assigned by the teacher or the principal

NOTE: Some lifting of students, equipment, or materials may be required

EVIDENCE OF PERFORMANCE:

- Adapted classroom activities to the students' abilities
- Assisted teacher with large and small student groups as well as with individual students
- Helped the teacher maintain classroom procedures, rules, and classroom management
- Attended to the personal and instructional needs of disabled students
- Maintained individual students' progress records
- Prepared instructional materials and resources

TERMS OF EMPLOYMENT:

Hours as assigned by the principal. Pay and benefits as determined by the human resources department. Initial probationary period is required.

Support Staff

Job Description: Secretary

Name: _____

Dept/School: _____

Date: _____

JOB GOAL:

To provide the school community with efficient secretarial services.

QUALIFICATIONS:

Minimum Training and Experience: Shall have a broad secretarial background with word processing, computer, and record-keeping knowledge. Competent in operation of standard office equipment. The individual in this position shall display good organizational, communication, teamwork, and interpersonal skills.

DESIRABLE TRAITS AND ATTITUDES:

- Has positive attitude toward job and clientele
- Conducts him- or herself in a professional and ethical manner
- Respects the values of confidentiality and integrity
- Has the ability to work independently, organize, and use time effectively
- Has the ability to work with frequent interruptions and adapt to changing circumstances
- Shows initiative, but is also willing to take and follow direction
- Works within the procedures and systems in the school community
- Works cooperatively with others

REPORTS TO:

The School Secretary will be responsible to the school administration.

PERFORMANCE RESPONSIBILITIES:

- Typing and ensuring accuracy of all documents and letters generated at the school level
- Receptionist and telephone answering
- Drafting general correspondence
- Keeping and maintaining school and student records
- Gathering information and preparation of reports
- Assist with inventory
- Assist with budget
- Maintain school accounts and textbook rentals and provide reports
- Banking duties, where appropriate
- Deliver and distribute school mail
- Prepare requisitions
- Check receipt of supplies and equipment
- Ensure that the office is maintained in a tidy and orderly manner
- Attend professional development activities to improve weaker skill areas
- Continue to improve expertise and job-related skills
- Implement other assignments and responsibilities as assigned by administration

NOTE 1: Some lifting and carrying may be required
NOTE 2: When a school has more than one secretary, the division of tasks will be at the principal's discretion

EVIDENCE OF PERFORMANCE:

- Worked effectively in a team enviroment
- Communicated effectively with students, staff, parents, and other members of the school community
- Effectively performed the clerical duties required
- Effectively performed the administrative support duties required at the school
- Demonstrated the abilities to multitask and prioritize workload
- Demonstrated the ability to maintain confidentiality

TERMS OF EMPLOYMENT:

Hours as assigned by the principal. Pay rates and benefits as determined by the Human Resources Department. Initial probationary period required.

Job Description: School Security Officer

Support Staff

Name: _____

Dept/School: _____

Date: _____

JOB GOALS:

1) To maintain constant surveillance of school campus to prevent disruptions, protect property, and ensure the safety of students and staff
2) To enforce the school district's rules and regulations
3) To provide a variety of assistance to persons using the facilities

DESIRABLE TRAITS, ABILITIES, AND ATTITUDES:

- Must possess a high school degree or equivalent
- Must have experience in law enforcement related field preferred
- Must have a solid knowledge of state and local law and the school board policy regarding discipline, basic institutional security measures, first aid, and CPR
- Must have ability to use good judgment when responding to security and safety violations and emergencies
- Should have demonstrated skill in the application of the principles of law enforcement and security and safety
- Should have a knowledge of technology as related to specific job functions
- Must have excellent oral and written communication skills
- Has positive attitude toward job and clientele
- Conducts him- or herself in a professional and ethical manner
- Respects the values of confidentiality and integrity
- Has the ability to work independently, organize, and use time effectively
- Has the ability to work with frequent interruptions and adapt to changing circumstances
- Shows initiative, but is also willing to take and follow direction
- Works within the procedures and systems in the school community
- Dresses appropriately for a school setting or in uniform, if required
- Works cooperatively with others and has the ability to establish and maintain effective working relationships with other employees and the public
- Must possess knowledge of occupational safety and health regulations

REPORTS TO:

The School Security Officer reports to the District's Chief Security Officer and to the Principal.

PERFORMANCE RESPONSIBILITIES:

- Work closely with school administration and staff regarding school activities
- Inspect school premises prior to opening and closing in regard to security
- Assist with the supervision of authorized student gatherings at various campus locations
- Assist with the school bus supervision before and after school
- Monitor students, campus, and parking lots and assists motorists to resolve vehicle problems
- Make hourly tours of campus to ensure that school and district policies are being enforced (cafeteria, restrooms, hallways, parking lots, etc.)
- Maintain daily activity log
- May provide escort and transportation services to ensure safety and physical well-being of students and staff
- Must be able to use technology that is critical in this job (i.e., hand and base radio, word processor, jiffy bar, etc.)
- Exhibit good judgment and initiative in emergency situations
- Establish and maintain good rapport with students
- Perform other duties as assigned by the Principal or designee

Support Staff

Job Description: School Security Officer (form continued)

Name: _____

Dept/School: _____

Date: _____

EVIDENCE OF PERFORMANCE:

- Observations and reports of problems
- Responds to requests in timely manner
- Number of complaints
- Timely submission of reports
- Thoroughly documented incident reports
- Relevant police reports
- Record of interventions
- Observation and anecdotal record
- Examples of willingness to respond to job demands
- Participation in graduate classes, workshops, or other specific training opportunities
- Demonstrates excellent interpersonal, time, conflict, and stress management skills

TERMS OF EMPLOYMENT:

School year with annual evaluation. Wages and benefits as outlined in the contract.

Job Description: Elementary Teacher

Teachers

Name: _____

Dept/School: _____

Date: _____

POSITION GOALS:

The teacher will build community; design and manage learning; communicate with students, families, and colleagues; and grow professionally. The teacher will also assist in other school programs as assigned.

QUALIFICATIONS:

- Must possess a valid teaching certificate
- Bachelor's degree (minimum) including all courses and state tests needed to meet credential requirements
- Personal resume
- Letters of recommendation
- Transcripts or verification of degree

DESIRABLE TRAITS AND ATTITUDES:

- Has a positive attitude
- Respects confidentiality and integrity
- Works well independently and also with a team
- Organized and uses time wisely
- Takes initiative, but also takes direction
- Shows professionalism and strong ethical behavior
- Dresses appropriately
- Positive role model for students
- Interpersonal and conflict resolution skills in dealing with students and parents

SUPERVISION:

- Responsible to principal
- Responsible for students
- Responsible to parents

MAJOR DUTIES AND RESPONSIBILITIES:

- Teaches all subjects utilizing the district curriculum, state benchmarks, and national standards
- Develops unit and lesson plans
- Provides individualized, small group, and large group instruction in order to meet the needs of each student
- Engages students in learning through best practice strategies
- Assesses students' academic and social growth
- Keeps appropriate records of student progress, prepares reports, and communicates progress with families
- Identifies students' special needs and works with other professional staff to best meet those needs
- Establishes, manages, and maintains procedures, routines, rules, and standards of student behavior
- Maintains a safe, clean, and comfortable classroom environment
- Selects and orders instructional supplies, materials, and resources
- Performs various noninstructional duties, such as attendance, lunch count, recess, etc.
- Attends professional development growth activities on a regular basis
- Participates cooperatively with the principal on the formative and summative performance appraisal process
- Supervises students both in and out of the classroom
- Participates in committee work, family activities, and sponsored student activites

Job Description: Secondary Teacher

Teachers

Name: _____

Dept/School: _____

Date: _____

POSITION GOALS:

The secondary teacher is a content specialist in one or two subjects. The ability to communicate complex ideas clearly is essential. Secondary teachers are responsible for all aspects of their students' classroom experiences as well as family partnerships and professional and personal growth.

QUALIFICATIONS:

- Must possess a valid teaching certificate
- Bachelor's degree (minimum) with major and minor in designated subject matter including all courses and tests needed to meet credential requirement
- Personal resume
- Letters of recommendation
- Transcripts or verification of degree

DESIRABLE TRAITS AND ATTITUDES:

- Possesses enthusiasm for subject matter and teaching adolescents
- Respects confidentiality and integrity
- Works well independently and also with a team
- Has strong communication and organizational skills
- Takes initiative, but also takes direction
- Shows professionalism and strong ethical behavior
- Dresses appropriately
- Positive role model for students
- Interpersonal and conflict resolution skills in dealing with students and parents

SUPERVISION:

- Responsible to principal
- Responsible for students
- Responsible to parents

MAJOR DUTIES AND RESPONSIBILITIES:

- Ability to help students achieve positive academic results
- Ability to inspire confidence and trust with students, parents, and colleagues
- Knowledge in adolescent cognitive development and learning styles
- Knowledge of content and best practices in designated disciplines
- Ability to organize classroom procedures and routines and manage student behavior
- Establishes high expectations
- Assesses students regularly and uses assessment data to improve instruction
- Collaborates with department colleagues and with colleagues from different disciplines to integrate learning
- Differentiates instruction for different types of learners
- Actively involved in professional development activities
- Provides families with information of student progress and classroom activities
- Uses technology to enhance curriculum
- Has the ability to diagnose and address student learning challenges

CONCLUSION

All of the job descriptions presented in this chapter are only templates—a place for you to start in creating your own job descriptions for your staff. However, they each include the key elements of a meaningful job description for a particular position that list responsibilities that can be measured and for which all employees can be held accountable, as well as identify areas that might need remediation and support.

SUPPORT STAFF BIBLIOGRAPHY

General Job Descriptions

National Education Association. (2003). *Doing our jobs.* Available at http://www.nea.org/esp/jobs

National Education Association. (2003). *102 ways educational support personnel are keeping the school environment healthy and safe.* Available at http://www.new.org/esp/resource/102 ways/htm

National Education Association. (2003). *101 ways educational support personnel are making a difference for public education.* Available at http://www.new.org/esp/resource/10 ways/htm

National Education Association. (2003). *Results-oriented job descriptions.* Available at http://www.nea.org/esp/jobs

Tennessean. (2003). *Some educational assistants must broaden qualifications.* Available at http://tennessean.com/education/archives/03/07/35282316.shtml

Workforce; HR Trends & Tools for Business Results. (2003). *A worksheet for measuring competencies.* Available at http://workforce.com/archive/article/23/35/27.php

Secretaries

Jean, Anna-Cain. (1998). *The organizer: Secrets and systems from the world's top executive assistants.* New York: Harper Collins.

Manhard, Stephen. (1998). *The goof-proofer: How to avoid the 41 most embarrassing errors in your speaking and writing.* New York: Fireside.

Marczely, Bernadette. (2001). *Supervision in education: A differentiated approach with legal perspectives.* Gaithersburg, MD: Aspen.

Merriam-Webster. (1993). *Merriam–Webster's secretarial handbook (3rd ed.).* Springfield, MA: Author.

Quibble, Zane K. (2000). *Administrative office management (7th ed.).* New York: Prentice Hall.

Sabin, William. (2001). *The Gregg reference manual (9th ed.).* New York: Glencoe McGraw Hill.

Spencer, John. (1995). *The professional secretary's handbook: The complete reference guide to today's office (3rd ed.).* New York: Houghton Mifflin.

Spencer, John. (1997). *The professional secretary's handbook: Communication skills.* New York: Barrons Educational Series.

Spencer, John. (1997). *The professional secretary's handbook: Management skills.* New York: Barrons Educational Series.

Strunk, William Jr. (2000). *The elements of style (4th ed.).* New York: Allyn & Bacon.

Paraprofessionals

Burke, Michelle Marie. (1996, October). *The valuable office professional: For administrative assistants, office managers, secretaries, and other support staff.* New York: AMACOM.

French, Nancy K. (2003). *Managing paraeducators in your school.* Thousand Oaks, CA: Corwin.

Lorenzo, David, & Twactman-Cullen, Diane. (March, 2000). *How to be a parapro: A comprehensive training manual for paraprofessionals.* Higganum, CT: Starfish Specialty Press.

Marczely, Bernadette. (2001). *Supervision in education: A differentiated approach with legal perspectives.* Gaithersburg, MD: Aspen.

Reeves, Douglas B. (2002). *Holistic accountability: Serving students, schools, and community.* Thousand Oaks, CA: Corwin.

Custodians

MacIha, John C. (2001, January). *Preventive maintenance guidelines for school facilities.* San Francisco: Robert S. Means.

Marczely, Bernadette. (2001). *Supervision in education: A differentiated approach with legal perspectives.* Gaithersburg, MD: Aspen.

Chapter Three

Teacher Performance Appraisal Coaching Tools

Teacher performance appraisal should be based on the belief that teachers are capable professionals. The ultimate goal of the performance appraisal process is to assist teachers to self-evaluate, reflect, and set goals for improvement. The district performance appraisal formative and summative tools should be a framework to support, encourage, and assist teachers' growth and development at different stages of their careers.

The primary purpose of teacher performance appraisal should be improved practice and must have as its main objectives improved student learning. However, it must be recognized that teaching is a complex process and that there is no single model of quality teaching. What every teacher needs in terms of skills and abilities is individual.

Performance appraisal should be developmental and should be predicated on the premise that the individual is accountable for the impact of his or her teaching performance. The instruments developed here make specific provision for both human and material resources to support improved practice. The responsibility for improvement does not lie solely with the individual teacher, but equally with the principal and the teacher.

As principals use the district's established instruments for formative and summative evaluation to help teachers improve, coaching tools are offered here to support district expectations in the following areas: building community, designing learning, managing learning, communicating, and growing professionally. Principals must be able to identify key components in each of these elements and to know if something is missing.

The Teacher Performance Appraisal Coaching Tools included in this chapter are grounded in an accurate reflection of the teacher's role with all its relevant responsibilities. Various models of professional teaching standards were used to shape these coaching tools. These nationally recognized models include the following: Charlotte Danielson's Four Domains of Teaching Responsibility (ASCD, 1996):

DOMAIN 1: PLANNING & PREPARATION	DOMAIN 2: THE CLASSROOM ENVIRONMENT
Demonstrating knowledge of content and pedagogy	Creating an environment of respect and rapport
Demonstrating knowledge of students	Establishing a culture for learning
Demonstrating knowledge of resources	Managing classroom procedures
Designing coherent instruction	Managing student behavior
Assessing student learning	Organizing physical space
DOMAIN 3: INSTRUCTION	DOMAIN 4: PROFESSIONAL RESPONSIBILITIES
Communicating clearly and accurately	Reflecting on teaching
Using questioning and discussion techniques	Maintaining accurate records
Engaging students in learning	Communicating with families
Demonstrating flexibility and responsiveness	Contributing to the school and district
	Growing and developing professionally
	Showing professionalism

Source: Adapted from Danielson, C. (1996). *Enhancing professional practice: A framework for teaching.* Alexandria, VA: Association for Supervision and Curriculum Development.

The National Board for Professional Teaching Standards (NBPTS):

PROPOSITION 1. Teachers who are committed to students and their learning should:

- Believe all students can learn
- Treat students equitably, recognizing individual differences and accounting for these differences in their practice
- Adjust their practice based on observation and knowledge of their students
- Understand how students develop and learn
- Develop students' respect for learning
- Develop students' self-esteem, character, respect for others

PROPOSITION 2. Teachers should know the subjects they teach and how to teach those subjects to students. They should:

- Understand how their subject is related to other disciplines
- Develop students' critical and analytical thinking skills
- Understand the preconceptions students have about a subject area
- Use multiple strategies to convey a concept
- Teach students how to pose and solve their own problems

PROPOSITION 3. Teachers must be responsible for managing and monitoring student learning. They should:

- Create environments that engage students and use time effectively
- Engage others (both students and colleagues) to assist them
- Be aware of ineffective and damaging instructional practices
- Set norms for social interaction

- Assess the growth of both individual students and the class as a whole
- Be able to explain a student's performance to parents

PROPOSITION 4. Teachers should think systematically about their practice and learn from experience. They should:

- Exemplify the virtues they seek to inspire in students
- Make decisions based not only on research, but also on their experience
- Be lifelong learners
- Think critically about their own practice and try employing new theories

PROPOSITION 5. Teachers should be members of learning communities. This means that they should:

- Work collaboratively with others to develop instructional policy, curriculum development, and staff development
- Evaluate school progress and the allocation of school resources relating to state and local educational objectives
- Have knowledge of special school and community resources for students and put these resources to work
- Work collaboratively with parents and engage their participation

Source: http://www.nbpts.org/standards/know_do/intro.html

The Interstate New Teacher Assessment and Support Consortium (INTASC) developed standards for what new teachers should be able to do. According to these standards, new teachers should:

1. Understand the central concepts, tools of inquiry, and structure of the disciplines taught; create learning experiences to make these concepts meaningful to students.

2. Understand how children learn and develop; provide learning opportunities that support their development.

3. Understand how students differ in their approaches to learning; create instructional opportunities adapted to diverse learners.

4. Understand and use variety of instructional strategies.

5. Create a learning environment that encourages positive social interaction, active engagement in learning, and self-motivation.

6. Use knowledge of communication techniques to foster active inquiry, collaboration, and supportive interaction.

7. Plan instruction based on knowledge of subject matter, students, the community, and curriculum goals.

8. Understand and use formal and informal assessment strategies.

9. Reflect on teaching.

10. Foster relationships with colleagues, parents, and agencies in the larger community.

Source: Adapted from Bliss, T., & Mazur, J. (2002). *K-12 teachers in the midst of reform.* Upper Saddle River, NJ: Merrill Prentice Hall.

It is no surprise that studies on teacher effectiveness and student achievement generally show that students who had the most effective teachers generally made greater gains in achievement than those who had less effective teachers. Effective teachers are characterized by having:

- good knowledge of pedagogy;
- good knowledge of content;
- commitment to individualize instruction, especially for at-risk students;
- a large repertoire of instructional strategies that are skillfully employed;
- strong verbal ability to convey lessons in clear and convincing ways;
- consistent and effective classroom management strategies;
- positive expectations about students' improvement;
- a willingness to continue their professional learning.

The Teacher Performance Appraisal Coaching Tools in this chapter were developed by combining, adapting and expanding ideas from each of the models and research listed above. **The Five Areas and Indicators of the Teacher Performance Appraisal Coaching Tools** are:

AREA 1: Building Community

Creating a Caring Environment

Demonstrating Enthusiasm

Planning Procedures and Routines

Developing Classroom Rules

Maintaining Behavioral Standards

Creating the Physical Environment

AREA 2: Designing Learning

Displaying Content Knowledge and Practice

Recognizing Individual Differences

Articulating Instructional Goals

Using Materials and Resources

Designing Units and Lessons

Assessing Learning

AREA 3: Managing Learning

Communicating Verbally and Nonverbally

Asking High-Quality Questions

Facilitating Learning Experiences

Giving Feedback

Making Instructional Adjustments

AREA 4: Communicating

Keeping Accurate Records

Communicating With Families

Serving and Advocating for Students

AREA 5: Growing Professionally

Reflecting on Teaching

Assuming Professional Leadership

Developing Professionally

The teacher performance appraisal coaching tools that follow have been designed for each of the indicators listed above. Each coaching tool has the following elements:

- **GOAL**—Indicates when the teacher is exceptional in this area
- **DESCRIPTION**—A further explanation of the goal
- **HELPFUL SUGGESTIONS**—Ideas that should help the teacher make improvements
- **TOOLS**—Templates that could be used with the teacher to help him or her improve (note: other tools could be designed by the principal)
- **FEEDBACK and REFLECTIONS**—Where additional ideas and suggestions could be recorded
- **REFERENCES**—Additional useful books and Web sites

These coaching tools could be given to a teacher at any time during the performance appraisal process. Perhaps an observation is conducted and the principal notices areas that need improvement. During a formative conference, the principal could share appropriate coaching tools with the teacher.

COLLECTING DATA DURING THE PERFORMANCE APPRAISAL PROCESS

Principals should be constantly collecting data to assist in discussions with the teacher during the performance appraisal process. Sources of information that could be used in each area include:

Area 1: Building Community

1. Student surveys

2. Parent surveys

3. Classroom observations—using some of the following techniques:
   - Scripting—a written record of exactly what is said in the classroom by the teacher and the students.
   - Recording who is talking to whom in the classroom—check to see if the teacher equally distributes opportunities to participate. Is the

teacher more frequently calling on students who are in the front, those who raise their hands, those who usually give correct responses? Are gender biases or other unintentional biases happening in the classroom?

- Recording who is on-task or off-task—obtain data on whether students are actively engaged in tasks during the lesson. Checking at regular intervals whether students are on-task, off-task, talking, out of seats, etc. This will help the teacher examine what factors influence student engagement. Was the instructional pace too fast or too slow? Was it before or after lunch? Were the students given too much time or not enough time for the required task?

- Recording teacher movement—record on a seating chart where the teacher positions himself or herself and where the teacher moves during the lesson. What effect did the teacher movement or lack of movement have on students in terms of learning, assistance, discipline, etc.?

Area 2: Designing Learning

1. Sample unit plans

2. Sample lesson plans

3. Teaching artifacts

Area 3: Managing Learning

1. Classroom observations

2. Videotaping lessons and reflecting on teacher and student behaviors

Area 4: Communicating

1. Phone logs

2. Newsletters

3. Web sites

4. "Open House" handouts

5. Parent surveys

Area 5: Growing Professionally

1. Interview

2. Reflection logs

3. Logs of professional activities

4. Copies of documents to which the teacher has contributed

5. Feedback from colleagues

REFERENCES

Darling-Hammond, L. (2000). Teacher quality and student achievement: A review of state policy evidence. *Educational Policy Analysis Archives, 8*(1).

Sanders, W. L., & Rivers, J. C. (1996). *Cumulative and residual effects of teachers on future student academic achievement.* Research Progress Report. Knoxville: University of Tennessee Valne-Added Research and Assessment Center.

TEACHER PERFORMANCE
APPRAISAL COACHING TOOLS

TEACHERS

AREA 1: Building Community—Concerns the teachers' skills in establishing an environment conducive to learning.

Indicators include:

- Creating a Caring Environment
- Demonstrating Enthusiasm
- Planning Procedures and Routines
- Developing Classroom Rules
- Maintaining Behavioral Standards
- Creating the Physical Environment

Creating a Caring Environment
Coaching Tool

Teachers

Name: _____

Dept/School: _____

Date: _____

GOAL:

The teacher will create a classroom environment where all members of the learning community demonstrate genuine, consistent care and respect for each other.

DESCRIPTIONS:

A classroom environment must be safe. Students must feel valued and treated with dignity. Teachers treat their students respectfully and teach their students to be responsible citizens.

HELPFUL SUGGESTIONS:

The use of a common language that helps students understand ethical values can guide students to act upon these values. Several organizations have materials and resources that can help find that common language that will assist in developing an environment of respect and rapport.

- The **Character Counts Coalition** uses six pillars of character—trustworthiness, Respect, Responsibility, Fairness, Caring, Citizenship. This organization offers a wide variety of materials and resources for classroom teachers. For more information, contact the Character Counts National Office at http://www.charactercounts.org.
- The **ITI Model for Brain-Compatible Learning,** by Susan Kovalik and Associates, uses Lifelong Guidelines and Lifeskills. Contact Susan Kovalik and Associates at http://www.kovalik.com.
- The book ***Tribes: A New Way of Learning and Being Together***, by Jeanne Gibbs (2000), provides step-by-step instructions on how to build a learning community and honors four agreements—attentive listening, appreciation/no put downs, mutual respect, and the right to pass. This book is also available in Spanish translation. For more information, go to http://www.tribes.com.
- The **Center for the Fourth and Fifth Rs** (respect and responsibility) offers extensive information on 11 principles of character education. The Web site for this organization is http://www.cortland.edu/c4n5rs/.
- The **Character Education Partnership (CEP)** is a nonpartisan coalition of organizations and individuals dedicated to developing moral character and civic virtue in our nation's youth as one means of creating a more compassionate and responsible society. Reach this organization at http://www.character.org/.

Creating a Caring Environment
Coaching Tool (form continued)

Teachers

Name: _____

Dept/School: _____

Date: _____

Students learn ethical values by discussing and observing them, by forming caring relationships, and by practicing positive social behaviors. What specific actions will you take to make sure your students understand, care about, and act upon the character qualities that you would like to promote in your classroom?

What list of character qualities would you like your students to develop this year (e.g. responsibility, respect, caring, self-control, etc.)?
How will you help your students **understand** these character qualities?
How will you help your students **care about** these character qualities?
What will you do to make sure your students **act upon** these character qualities?

FOLLOW-UP/REFLECTION:

What would your school community add to your list of character qualities that could be a list that your entire building would embrace?

_____

_____

REFERENCES:

Gibbs, J. (2000). *Tribes: A new way of learning and being together*. Windsor, CA: Center Source Systems, LLC.

Kovalik, S., & Olson, K. (2002). *Exceeding expectations: A user's guide to implementing brain research in the classroom*. Covington, WA: Susan Kovalik and Associates.

Teachers

Demonstrating Enthusiasm
Coaching Tool

Name: _____

Dept/School: _____

Date: _____

GOAL:

The teacher will demonstrate enthusiasm for the content being taught. Students reflect this attitude through active participation, curiosity, and attention to detail and by having pride in their work.

DESCRIPTION:

Classrooms with an enthusiastic culture for learning are places where the atmosphere is open and positive. Students are given frequent, early, and positive feedback on tasks that are neither too easy or too difficult. Students feel that they are valuable members of the learning community. The teacher sets the tone for the learning culture by being an enthusiastic instructor who is well-organized and who takes a genuine interest in students and what they learn.

HELPFUL SUGGESTIONS:

Effective learning in the classroom depends on the teacher's ability to inspire, challenge, and stimulate his or her students. Research has shown that the teacher's enthusiasm is a major contributor to student motivation. A teacher's enthusiasm comes from confidence, excitement about the subject matter, and a genuine pleasure in teaching.

You can determine how enthusiastic you appear to students when you are teaching by paying attention to the following behaviors:

- **Eyes:** Eyes need to light up frequently. Sometimes, open eyes wide with eyebrows raised. Eye contact is a key when delivering instruction since it helps you make a connection with the students. Try to pretend you are having a conversation with individual students as you deliver instruction. Look into students' eyes for 3-5 seconds. If it is longer than this, students will feel uncomfortable.

- **Voice:** You need to look and sound enthused in order to motivate the students. Learn to vary the pitch or inflection in order to keep students awake and attentive. Make sure the tone is pleasant, natural, sincere, vivacious, and easily heard. Avoid monotone. Avoid using filler words. If this is difficult for you, consider joining a Toastmasters International Club. For more information, check the following Web site: http://www.toastmasters.org.

- **Gestures and Body Movement:** Move around the classroom with purpose, sometimes walking rapidly, changing pace, unpredictably stopping to emphasize a point, etc. This helps to express your energy and enthusiasm. Avoid repeating movements such as pacing and shifting your weight from one foot to another. These are distracting and may show students that you are nervous. Use hand gestures to show size, direction, or location or to emphasize points or compare and contrast. Gestures are also used to show openness.

- **Facial Expressions:** Vary your facial expression, allowing your expressions to match your content. Smile often.

Demonstrating Enthusiasm
Coaching Tool (form continued)

Teachers

Name: _____

Dept/School: _____

Date: _____

- **Word Selection:** Use colorful, highly descriptive words that paint a vivid pictures. Select precisely the right words required to communicate your ideas clearly and vividly. Avoid lengthy words and sentences and jargon.

- **Sincerity:** Convince the students of your earnestness, sincerity, and conviction on a subject you thoroughly understand. Advocate a point of view on which you feel strongly and learn how to convey your true feelings to the students. Be quick to be accepting, offer praise and encouragement, or ask for clarifications. Let students know you don't carry a grudge. Avoid sarcasm. Let students know that this is a safe environment for taking risks.

- **Overall Energy:** Be exuberant and show vitality. Do whatever it takes to make learning interesting and fun.

"The mediocre teacher tells.
The good teacher explains.
The superior teacher demonstrates.
The great teacher inspires."
—William Arthur Ward

You can determine how enthusiastic you appear to your students by videotaping one or two lessons and rating yourself. Make sure you evaluate more than one lesson. Try to change areas where you need improvement by practicing behaviors listed in the "high" categories.

Rate yourself for each category along the continuum below. 1 = low and 7 = high.

	Low						High
	1	2	3	4	5	6	7
Eyes							

Look bored. Seldom open wide with raised eyebrows. Eye contact avoided.

Look bright. Often open wide with raised eyebrows. Eye contact with many students.

	Low						High
	1	2	3	4	5	6	7
Voice							

Monotone. Little variance in pitch and inflection. Many filler words.

Great and sudden changes in tone and pitch.

Demonstrating Enthusiasm
Coaching Tool (form continued)

Teachers

Name: _____

Dept/School: _____

Date: _____

Gestures & Body Movement

Low 1	2	3	4	5	6	High 7

Seldom moved from one spot or from sitting. Sometimes paces. Few gestures.

Uses movement and gestures to emphasize points.

Facial Expression

Low 1	2	3	4	5	6	High 7

Deadpan or frowning. Little smiling.

Many different positive expressions. Frequent smiles.

Word Selection

Low 1	2	3	4	5	6	High 7

Few descriptors or adjectives. Simple expressions.

Colorful, descriptive words. Short, but meaningful sentences.

Sincerity

Low 1	2	3	4	5	6	High 7

Little indication of acceptance or encouragement. Sarcastic.

Accepting. Offers frequent praise and encouragement. Asks for clarifications.

Overall Energy

Low 1	2	3	4	5	6	High 7

Inactive, dull, sluggish.

Exuberant. Shows vitality.

7 - 19	indicates **unenthusiatic**
20 - 36	indicates **moderate enthusiasm**
37 - 49	indicates **very high level of enthusiasm**

**Demonstrating Enthusiasm
Coaching Tool** (form continued)

Teachers

Name: _____

Dept/School: _____

Date: _____

FOLLOW-UP/REFLECTION:

What can you do to make sure that students have good attitudes and perceptions about learning in your classroom?

_____

_____

REFERENCES:

Jensen, E. (2003). *Tools for engagement: Managing emotional states for learner success.* San Diego, CA: The Brain Store.

McCarty, H., & Siccone, F. (2000). *Motivating your students: Before you can teach them, you have to reach them.* Boston, MA: Pearson, Allyn & Bacon.

Mendler, A. N. (1992). *What do I do when . . . ? How to achieve discipline with dignity in the classroom.* Bloomington, IN: National Education Service.

Mendler, A. N. (2001). *Motivating students who don't care: Successful techniques for educators.* Bloomington, IN: National Education Service.

Planning Procedures and Routines
Coaching Tool

Teachers

Name: _____

Dept/School: _____

Date: _____

GOAL:

The teacher will design procedures and routines that allow students to learn, be successful, and function effectively in the classroom. Procedures will be explained to students and students will be given opportunites to practice.

DESCRIPTION:

Procedures can be methods, processes, or sets of expected behaviors for how things are to be done in the classroom. Procedures help to maintain consistency in the classroom and provide students with a sense of security. The average classroom needs between 30 and 50 procedures to funtion smoothly.

HELPFUL SUGGESTIONS:

Well-designed procedures should be:
- Unique to each type of activity
- Clearly defined and positively phrased
- Explained and demonstrated as necessary
- Discussed with students on the rationale and application of the procedure
- Practiced
- Reviewed, retaught, and reinforced for at least three weeks until students understand and function automatically

A wide variety of tasks, activities, and transitions demand that teachers design procedures.
Listed below are just a few areas that need procedures:
- Beginning of class
- Taking attendance
- Transitions in the classroom
- Independent work
- Collaborative group work
- Use of materials and equipment
- Use of restrooms
- Going to lockers
- Dismissal
- Student attention during presentations
- Behavior during interruptions
- Getting the teacher's attention
- Collecting homework

EXAMPLE OF A WRITTEN PROCEDURE:

Heading on Papers to Be Turned In

- All information should be in the upper right-hand corner.
- First Line: Your name (first and last) and your roll call number.
- Second Line: Class name and hour (Example: "Biology 3rd Hour").
- Third Line: Name of assignment (Example: Essay on Elements in My Environment)
- Fourth Line: Date: Day of week, month, day of month (Example: Thursday September 22)

Planning Procedures and Routines
Coaching Tool (form continued)

Teachers

Name: _____

Dept/School: _____

Date: _____

Use this template to make a list of the classroom procedures you need to design. Group them under the headings provided.

Starting the Day:	Classroom Materials:
Grading:	Homework:
Movement Within the Classroom:	Movement out of the Classroom:
Classroom Visitors:	Parental Involvement and Contact:

FOLLOW-UP/REFLECTION:

How did the establishment of well-written and practiced procedures enhance the learning for students as individuals and as a group?

_____

_____

REFERENCES:

Kaufeldt, M. (1999). *Begin with the brain: Orchestrating the learner-centered classroom.* Tuscon, AZ: Zephyr Press.

Yanoff, J. C. (2000). *The classroom teacher's trouble-shooting handbook: Practical solutions to problems with students, adults, and procedures.* Chicago: Arthur Coyle Press.

Yanoff, J. C. (2002). *The excellent teacher's handbook: Exercises to take your teaching to a higher level.* Chicago: Arthur Coyle Press.

**Developing Classroom Rules
Coaching Tool**

Teachers

Name: _____

Dept/School: _____

Date: _____

GOAL:

The teacher will develop classroom rules that are guidelines or benchmarks that assist students in examining their behavior.

DESCRIPTION:

Classroom rules are usually limited to three to six. They are stated in general language that encourages students to take responsibility for their behavior. Rules communicate expectations and form the basis for catching students being good. Rules are the value system reflecting the culture—or desired culture—of a learning environment.

HELPFUL SUGGESTIONS:

- Establish rules the first day of school
- Explain the importance of rules in a positive manner
- Involve students in the development of classroom rules. This will help them feel a sense of ownership. However, often student rules and consequences are too strict and need to be monitored by the teacher
- Keep rules to a minimum
- Keep wording simple
- State rules positively
- Rules should be broad enough to cover a wide range of behaviors
- Some rules may need to be specific to address situations unique to a certain classroom or subject
- Rules should be relevant, clear, and concise
- Post the rules promptly and prominently in the classroom
- Periodically remind students of the rules

Examples of classroom rules:

- Appropriate behavior is expected
- Be prompt
- Help maintain a safe environment
- Be prepared for class
- Be polite
- Respect yourself and others
- Be productive
- Keep your supplies organized
- Complete all homework
- Solve conflicts nonviolently
- Follow teacher requests
- Demonstrate respect
- Allow learning to take place without disruption
- Take responsibility for your actions

Developing Classroom Rules
Coaching Tool (form continued)

Teachers

Name: _____

Dept/School: _____

Date: _____

Classroom Rules Checklist and Action Plan			
Item:	Yes	No	Plan of Action/Resources Needed
1. Have you established your classroom rules?			
2. Does the number of rules exceed six?			
3. Are the rules stated with positive wording?			
4. Are the rules prominently displayed in the classroom?			
5. Have you defined positive and negative consequences for following or not following the rules?			
6. Have you planned how to teach and demonstrate the ways to follow the rules?			
7. Are parents informed of the rules?			

FOLLOW-UP/REFLECTION:

How do I encourage students to internalize classroom rules and become self-directed learners?

_____

_____

REFERENCES:

Canter, L., & Canter, M. (2002). *Assertive discipline: positive behavior management for today's classroom.* Canter and Associates, Inc.

Fay, J., & Funk, D. (1998). *Teaching with love and logic: Taking control of the classroom.* Golden, CO: Love and Logic Institute, Inc.

Jones, V. F., & Jones, L. S. (2003). *Comprehensive classroom management: Creating communities of support and solving problems* (7th ed.). Boston: Allyn & Bacon.

**Maintaining Behavioral Standards
Coaching Tool**

Teachers

Name: _____

Dept/School: _____

Date: _____

GOAL:

The teacher will make sure that conduct standards are clear to students and students exhibit appropriate behavior. The teacher's response to any misbehavior is appropriate, successful, and respectful of the students' dignity.

DESCRIPTION:

A classroom that is efficiently and respectfully managed has clear, agreed-upon expectations of conduct and well-defined, appropriate consequences for any misbehavior. Consistency is key to the success of the management plan.

HELPFUL SUGGESTIONS:

- Once rules have been set, discussed, posted, and rehearsed, students also need to be aware of the consequences they will face if they make bad decisions. The consequences for breaking classroom rules should be the same for all students each time a rule is broken. Consequences can be positive (rewards) or negative (penalties).

- Consequences should fit the offense. They should be relevant and reasonable. Harsh consequences do not accomplish much except for breeding hatred. When selecting consequences, start with less intensive interventions. Consider moving to a more intensive or restrictive consequence only if the milder alternative proves ineffective.

- Reward systems can offer a way for student to benefit from good behavior. However, choose rewards as carefully as you choose consequences. They should be simple and meaningful to students. A positive classroom will accomplish much more than a classroom that is filled with negativism.

- Try to give students choices. This help them have power to make a good choice. For example: 1. You may leave the room and go to . . . a preselected place. 2. You may stay here and make changes in your personal choices. 3. You may stay in the room, but change your seat to an area where you agree there will be fewer problems. Which do you choose?

- If the emotional or physical well being of a student is at risk, then the offender should be removed from the room—no choices.

- Some students may need individual behavioral plans. If this must happen, find people who can help you set the plan—parents, principal, counselor, psychologist, social worker, etc. It should be discussed with the student that there will be consequences for bad behavior, but if the student has some input and something to work for, you may find success with an individual behavior modification plan.

- Parents should be provided with a copy of the rules, procedures, consequences, and rewards Rules, procedures, consequences, and rewards should be consistent with your team or grade-level colleagues.

Maintaining Behavioral Standards
Coaching Tool (form continued)

Teachers

Name: _____

Dept/School: _____

Date: _____

List your rules and the reasonable and relevant consequence that will be assigned if students make bad decisions.

Rule	Reasonable/Relevant Consequence
1.	
2.	
3.	
4.	
5.	

FOLLOW-UP/REFLECTION:

How do you establish and consistently maintain standards for behavior that reflect students' developmental and personal needs?

_____

_____

REFERENCES:

Evertson, C., Emmer, E., & Worsham, M. (2000). *Classroom management for secondary teachers*. Needham Heights, MA: Allyn & Bacon.

Kohn, A. (1993). *Punished by rewards*: The trouble with gold stars, incentive plans, A's, praise, and other bribes. Boston: Houghton Mifflin.

McEwan, B. (2000). *The art of classroom management: Effective practices for building equitable learning communities*. Upper Saddle River, NJ: Merrilll/Prentice Hall.

Sapon-Shevin, M. (1999). *Because we can save the world*. Boston: Allyn & Bacon.

Creating the Physical Environment
Coaching Tool

Teachers

Name: _____

Dept/School: _____

Date: _____

GOAL:

The teacher will arrange the classroom in ways that promote efficient learning and minimize behavior problems.

DESCRIPTION:

A safe and effective classroom must be arranged so that students will be able to see and hear instruction and have efficient access to learning materials. The teacher should be able to easily monitor students. The classroom should also be flexible to allow for different types of learning activities and different learning styles.

NOTE:

Organizing the physical space of the ideal classroom is no easy task considering the number of variables that must be taken into consideration. Such things as class size, course level, delivery method, discipline, teaching style, and learning objectives all must be taken into account.

HELPFUL SUGGESTIONS:

- **Student Desks/Tables**
  - Students should be seated so that their attention is directed toward the teacher. However, this could take the shape of different configurations, such as cooperative groups of four or U-shaped designs
  - Students should be able to clearly see boards, screens, presentation and display areas
  - Change seating arrangements based on the instructional objective
  - High traffic areas should be free of congestion
  - Develop places for group learning—breakout spaces, alcoves, table groupings to facilitate social learning
  - Students need their personal space. The classroom should allow students to create and modify their own personalized area; the perception of personal control lowers stress, enhances engagement, and provides a safe "home base" from which the student can explore
  - When arranging the classroom furniture, arrange seating to accommodate any students with special needs

- **Environmental Preferences (temperature, lighting, and noise level)**
  - Create both well-lit and dimly lit areas
  - Provide opportunities for students to move around
  - Establish some informal furniture arrangements
  - Establish both active and passive places; students need places for reflection and to retreat away from others for intrapersonal time as well as places for active engagement for the interpersonal intelligence
  - Try to refrain from keeping a classroom too cool or too warm
  - Caring for live plants can give the classroom a warm, comforting feel

**Creating the Physical Environment
Coaching Tool** (form continued)

Teachers

Name: _____

Dept/School: _____

Date: _____

- **Classroom Materials**
  - Frequently used materials should be visibly stored and accessible
  - Separate student materials from teacher materials
  - Students should be able to quickly and easily find their work and begin working
  - The teacher should have a place near the front of the room so that learning materials can be organized and available prior to the lesson
  - Develop consistent areas where students pick up corrected work and turn in completed work
  - Supplies should be clearly labeled so that materials can be put back where they belong

- **Bulletin Boards and Displays**
  - Displays created by students have more connection and owership
  - Topics should be current and reflect what is being taught
  - Displays should change as the class moves on to new topics
  - Make sure that materials placed on the bulletin boards and displays are neat, legible, and correct
  - Especially in elementary classrooms, each student in the class should have work on display
  - Bulletin boards may be used to aid in instruction
  - Bulletin boards are a good place to post reminders or frequently used print material such as rules, procedures, or schedules
  - From an artistic point of view, think of colors that harmonize and balance one another
  - Think about the cultural backgrounds of the students when designing bulletin boards and displays

- **Technology**
  - With the advancement in technology, equipment being used by teachers is ever changing. The following Internet site contains a tool that allows a teacher to create an ideal floorplan and hardware setup for the classroom (Design your own classroom with Teaching Matter, Inc.): http://www.atschool.org/materials/classroom/buildaclass/.

Creating the Physical Environment
Coaching Tool (form continued)

Teachers

Name: _____

Dept/School: _____

Date: _____

Taking ideas from "Helpful Suggestions" design a classroom floorplan that maximizes classroom space and reflects your individual teaching style.

FOLLOW-UP/REFLECTION:

How does this classroom arrangement facilitate learning for exploration, discovery, experimentation, and mastery?

_____

_____

REFERENCES:

Jensen, E. (2003). *Environments for learning*. San Diego, CA: The Brain Store.

Schechter, H. (2001). *Let go of clutter*. New York: McGraw-Hill.

TEACHER PERFORMANCE
APPRAISAL COACHING TOOLS

TEACHERS

AREA 2: Designing Learning—Includes the understanding of concepts to be taught, knowledge of individual learning differences, designing instruction, and assessments.

Indicators include:

- Displaying Content Knowledge and Practice
- Recognizing Individual Differences
- Articulating Instructional Goals
- Using Materials and Resources
- Designing Units and Lessons
- Assessing Learning

**Displaying Content Knowledge and Practices
Coaching Tool**

Teachers

Name: _____

Dept/School: _____

Date: _____

GOAL:

The teacher will display extensive content knowledge and demonstrate a commitment to the continuing pursuit of such knowledge. This will include continually searching for best practices to teach content most effectively.

DESCRIPTION:

Evolving knowledge of content and pedagogy can be achieved by learning about new knowledge and best practices within specific disciplines and by participating in professional growth activities.

HELPFUL SUGGESTIONS:

Web sites for content specific professional organizations for educators:

Art
National Art Education Association
http://www.naea-reston.org

English/Reading
International Reading Association
http://www.reading.org

*Teachers of English
to Speakers of Other Languages*
http://www.tesol.org

The National Council of Teachers of English
http://www.ncte.org

Languages
American Association of Teachers of French
http://frenchteachers.org

American Association of Teachers of German
http://aatg.org

*The American Association of Teachers
of Spanish and Portuguese*
http://aatsp.org

*American Council on the Teaching of
Foreign Languages*
http://actfl.org

Library
American Library Association
http://www.ala.org

Mathematics
National Council of Teachers of Mathematics
http://www.nctm.org

Music
Music Teachers National Association
http://www.mtna.org

National Association for Music Education
http://www.mtna.org

Physical Education
*The National Association for Sport and
Physical Education*
http://www.aahperd.org/naspe/

Science
National Association of Biology Teachers
http://www.nabt.org

National Science Teachers Association
http://www.nsta.org

Social Studies
The National Council for the Social Studies
http://www.ncss.org

Special Needs/Gifted
Council for Exceptional Children
http://www.cec.sped.org

Technology
*Association for Educational
Communications and Technology*
http://www.aect.org

*International Society
for Technology in Education*
http://www.iste.org

Displaying Content Knowledge & Practices
Coaching Tool (form continued)

Teachers

Name: _____

Dept/School: _____

Date: _____

Some miscellaneous Web sites for professional educators:

American Association of School Teachers
http://www.aasa.org

American Association of School Administrators
http://www.aasa.org

American Educational Research Association
http://www.aera.net

Association for Supervision and Curriculum
Development
http://www.ascd.org

The Knowledge Loom: Focus on Best Practice
http://knowledgeloom.org

National Association for the Education of Young
Children
http://naeyc.org

National Association for Gifted Children
http://nagc.org

National Middle School Association
http://www.nmsa.org

National Board for Professional Teaching Standards
http://www.nbpts.org

Phi Delta Kappa International
http://www.pdkintl.org

Joining a professional organization helps you stay informed, allows you to network with others in the field, and provides opportunities to learn and grow. Memberships may also benefit you by providing liability insurance, special discounts, and subscriptions to newsletters, scholarly journals and other publications.

Name: _____

Name of organization you would like to join: _____

Cost: $_____

Address where membership and publications will be sent:

_____

(address)   (city)   (state)   (zip code)

Reason(s) for wanting to join this organization:

FOLLOW-UP/REFLECTION:

How will you use the information you gain by joining this organization? How will you share this information with your colleagues?

_____

_____

REFERENCE:

For a complete listing of regional, state, and national organizations, see http://www.lpi.usra.edu/education/OSS/a-z.html#A

Recognizing Individual Differences
Coaching Tool

Teachers

Name: _____

Dept/School: _____

Date: _____

GOAL:

The teacher will demonstrate a solid comprehension of students' varied learning profiles, ability, or readiness levels, interests, and cultural heritage and will recognize what implications these have for instructional planning. The teacher will also display knowledge of the typical developmental characteristics of the students' age group.

DESCRIPTION:

Students vary tremendously in intellectual, social, and emotional readiness. Their talents, interests, and preferred approaches to learning are also vast. While planning learning activities the skilled teacher will help students build on their strengths and will accommodate their special needs.

HELPFUL SUGGESTIONS:

- "Brain research suggest[s] three broad and interrelated principles that point clearly to the need for differentiated instruction, that is, classrooms responsive to students' varying readiness levels, varying interests, and varying learning profiles" (Kalbfleisch and Tomlinson, 1998, pp. 53-54).
- The key to a differentiated classroom is that all students are regularly offered choices and students are matched with tasks compatible with their individual learner profiles.
- Curriculum should be differentiated in three areas:
  1. Content: multiple options for taking in information
  2. Process: multiple options for making sense of the ideas
  3. Product: multiple option for expressing what they know
- One way to meet the needs of differing readiness levels would be to develop tiered assignments. Tiered assignments are multiple versions of an assignment that allow students to build on their prior knowledge and that prompt their continued learning.
- Another way to differentiate is by accommodating individual learning approaches. Howard Gardner identified individual talents or aptitudes in his Multiple Intelligences theories.
- Interest surveys are often used for determining student interest. Brainstorming for subtopics within a curriculum concept and using semantic webbing to explore interesting facets of the concept is another effective tool to help students determine their interests.

Recognizing Individual Differences
Coaching Tool (form continued)

Teachers

Name: _____

Dept/School: _____

Date: _____

DESIGNING TIERED ASSIGNMENTS:

1. Make sure all tiered activities are introduced with the same level of enthusiasm and interest
2. Take care to give different work, not simply more or less work, for different tiers
3. Make sure that all students are equally involved and active
4. Ensure that all activities are equally appealing and desirable

	Offers **basic level** comprehension and performance expectations	Allows further depth of exploration and **mid-level** activities	Challenges in-depth understanding shown in **high-level** processes
What is the **objective** for each group?			
What **instructional strategies** will be used for each readiness level, learning profile, or interest?			
What **learning activities** will be used for each readiness level, learning profile, or interest?			
What will be the end **result or product** for each readiness level, learning profile, or interest?			

FOLLOW-UP/REFLECTION:

During a specific unit, how will you tier curriculum, instruction, and assessment for different readiness levels? By learning profile? For differing interests?

_____

_____

REFERENCES:

Gregory, G. H. (2003). *Differentiated instructional strategies in practice: Training, implementation, and supervision.* Thousand Oaks, CA: Corwin.

Kalbfleish, M. L., & Tomlinson, C. A. (1998). Teach me, teach my brain: A call for differentiated classrooms, *Educational Leadership*, November, 52-55.

Melin, J. (2001). *Passport to learn: Projects to challenge high-potential learners.* Tucson, AZ: Zephyr Press.

Tomlinson, C. A. (2002). *How to differentiate instruction in a mixed ability classroom.* Alexandria, VA: Association of Supervision and Curriculum Development.

Articulating Instructional Goals
Coaching Tool

Teachers

Name: _____

Dept/School: _____

Date: _____

GOAL:

The teacher will clearly articulate how goals establish high expectations and relate to curriculum frameworks and standards. All goals are clear, are written in the form of student learning, and can be accurately assessed.

DESCRIPTION:

When establishing goals, the teacher must take the following into account: the district curriculum, state and/or national standards and benchmarks and also the expectations of the community. Instructional goals clearly state what students will learn and be able to do.

HELPFUL SUGGESTIONS:

Standards:

- Teaching to standards is a top priority in education today. Successful change occurs when all aspects of the school curriculum are linked to standards through a purposeful, coherent system of processes and products.

- Links to standards listed by subject area and by state are found at the following Web site: http://edstandards.org/Standards.html#Subject

Curriculum Mapping:

- Curriculum mapping is a process for collecting data that identifies the core content, processes, and assessment used in curriculum for each subject area in order to improve communication and instruction in all areas of the curriculum. Curriculum mapping would be important do to if it is unclear if your school or district curriculum is aligned with state and national standards. By carefully looking at the maps, educators can fix gaps and repetitions, look for potential areas of integration, and consider ways to upgrade teaching goals, strategies, and materials.

- Heidi Hayes Jacobs has developed exceptional materials to help teachers, schools, and districts map their curriculum.

- *Mapping the Big Picture: Integrating Curriculum and Assessment K-12* (1997) describes a seven-step process for creating and working with curriculum maps, from data collection to ongoing curriculum review.

- *Curriculum Mapping: Charting the Course for Content* (1999) is a videotape series that shows actual teachers creating curriculum maps and using them to increase student achievement.

- Both of these resources are available through The Association for Supervision and Curriculum Development: http://ascd.org.

Articulating Instructional Goals
Coaching Tool (form continued)

Teachers

Name: _____

Dept/School: _____

Date: _____

Dimensions of Learning Model

- *Dimensions of Learning* (Marzano & Pickering, 1997) is a comprehensive model that can help educators link **content standards** (dealing with the academic knowledge and skills belonging to specific disciplines), **higher-level thinking skills, and lifelong learning standards** (dealing with knowledge and skills that cut across all disciplines and are applicable to life outside the classroom). This model is helpful to use when developing instructional goals.

Look up the state standards for your grade level. Choose one standard and develop instructional goals that will help your students extend or refine their knowledge about this standard and use the knowledge from this standard in a meaningful way.

Content Standard:
How will students extend and refine their knowledge for this standard?
How will students use the knowledge from this standard in a meaningful way?

FOLLOW-UP/REFLECTION:

Who is currently teaching what standards in your school? What is the nature of instruction? Who is currently assessing what standards? By what means?

_____

_____

REFERENCES:

Jacobs, H. H. (1997). *Mapping the big picture: Integrating curriculum and assessment K-12.* Alexandria, VA: ASCD.

Jacobs, H. H. (1999). *Curriculum mapping: Charting the course for content.* Alexandria, VA: ASCD.

Marzano, R. J., & Pickering, D. J. (1997). *Dimensions of learning, teacher's manual* (2nd ed.) Alexandria, VA: ASCD.

**Using Materials and Resources
Coaching Tool**

Teachers

Name: _____

Dept/School: _____

Date: _____

GOAL:

The teacher will take steps to utilize school and district materials and resources and will actively seek out additional resources that will be used to enhance instruction.

DESCRIPTION:

Besides using resources provided by the school and district, teachers enhance their students' learning experiences by making use of a wide variety of resources including field trips to local events and businesses. Teachers also draw from a wide variety of human resources, from experts within the classroom community (students and parents), to those from the larger business and civic world. Technology–based resources are also effective.

HELPFUL SUGGESTIONS:

Internet Suggestions:

- The World Wide Web has thousands of useful resources for teachers. Including (to name a few):
  - Units, lesson plans, and teaching tips
  - Worksheets, graphic organizers, quizzes, and tests
  - Puzzles, flashcards, and games
  - Forms, checklists, clip art, newsletters, and calendars

- One of the better resources found on the World Wide Web are WebQuests. WebQuests are inquiry-oriented activities in which some or all of the information that learners interact with comes from resources on the Internet (Dodge, 1997).
  - Excellent examples of WebQuests can be found at: http://webquest.org/

Community Involvement Suggestions:

- Barbara Lewis' book (1998), *A Kid's Guide To Social Action* is a wonderful resource that teaches students how to actively engage in positive social change. The books includes ready to copy resources and tools such as various forms for making phone calls, letter writing, interviewing, speech making, surveying, fundraising, and media coverage. Addresses, phone numbers, and Web sites are included for social action groups and government resources.

Video Suggestions:

Using a variation of a standard lesson plan, a specific instructional plan should be in place before, during and after students view instructional videos.

Before – State how the video is connected to the curriculum.

Before – Do a previewing activity that sets the tone for the video.

Before – Present questions or have students formulate questions before viewing the video.

During – Pause the video at appropriate places to have students do an activity, make a prediction, or answer the previewing questions.

After – Discuss the key points of the video.

After – Do a meaningful follow-up activity.

After – Evaluate the lesson and note the things that could be changed or improved.

Using Materials and Resources
Coaching Tool (form continued)

Teachers

Name: _____

Dept/School: _____

Date: _____

Always preview videos to make the viewing of the program more meaningful for students. As you are planning the video–based lesson, decide what you will do.

How is the video connected to the curriculum?
What previewing activity will students do?
What questions will be answered as students watch the video?
At what point will the video be paused for questions, predictions, or activities?
What will be asked during the post-viewing discussion?
What activities will reinforce the concepts presented in the video?
Was the video used as effectively as possible? What worked well? What could be changed?

FOLLOW-UP/REFLECTION:

Brainstorm a list of experts, field trips, videos, WebQuests, Web sites, resource books, etc., that you can use for an upcoming unit.

_____

_____

REFERENCES:

Dodge, B. (1997). *Some thoughts about WebQuests*. San Diego State University. Available at http://edweb.sdsu.edu/courses/edtec596/about_webquests.html

Lewis, B. (1998). *A kid's guide to social action: How to solve the social problems you choose—and turn creative thinking into positive action*. Minneapolis, MN: Free Spirit Publishing.

Reeves, E. (n.d.). *7-step lesson plan for using instructional TV in the classroom*. San Francisco, CA: KQED-TV. Available at http://www.unctv.org/education/tvforteachers/usingtv00.html#teacher

**Designing Units and Lessons
Coaching Tool**

Teachers

Name: _____

Dept/School: _____

Date: _____

GOAL:

The teacher will create a series of learning activities within an instructional unit. This sequence will be logical and will engage students in meaningful learning activities.

DESCRIPTION:

When planning units and lessons, the teacher pays close attention to curriculum standards and "big ideas" then designs meaningful assessments and activities. The teacher has carefully planned adequate time allocation for the units and lessons and has considered all important resources and materials.

HELPFUL SUGGESTIONS:

The goal of the questions listed under each step shown below is to assist you in thinking about what you want to teach during this unit and why; to help you be thoughtful about the choices you make about topics, activities/tasks, and materials; to assist you in considering how to best organize students for the activities you choose; and to help you monitor students' progress toward the learning goals you have for the unit.

- **Step 1: Address the following questions about the unit goals (content and cognitive):**
  - Why are you teaching this unit?
  - What do you want students to know and be able to do?
  - What knowledge, skills, strategies, and attitudes do you want students to gain?
  - What important content and concepts will students learn?
  - How can connections be made to previous and future skills and concepts?
  - What are the time and resource constraints?
  - How available are the necessary materials and resources?
  - What do you know about this topic and what do you need to learn and work on in order to teach it?

- **Step 2: Address the following question about linking to curriculum standards:**
  - What district curriculum guidelines, state frameworks, or national standards will be addressed?

- **Step 3: Address the following questions about the "big idea" for this unit:**
  - What "big idea" questions will be asked to help students focus on the most important aspects of this unit?
  - Why would students care about or why would they want to know about this topic?
  - Why do students need to know this information?

Designing Units and Lessons
Coaching Tool (form continued)

Teachers

Name: _____

Dept/School: _____

Date: _____

- **Step 4: Address the following questions about assessment:**
  - How will you know that the students have reached the unit goals?
  - What types of assessment tools will be used?
  - How will students assess themselves?
  - How will you keep track of and record students' progress?
  - What kind of culminating activity will give students a chance to consolidate and demonstrate what they have learned and how will you evaluate this?

- **Step 5: Address the following questions about learning connections:**
  - What student needs, interests, and prior learning are foundations for this unit?
  - What anticipated conceptual difficulties might students have?
  - How can cross-curricular connections be made between various subjects during the unit?
  - What "real-world" connection can be made during the unit?
  - What sequence will provide for optimal connections between lessons?

- **Step 6: Address the following questions about learning activities/tasks:**
  - What engaging and essential learning activities will be developed?
  - How will knowledge and skills build from simple to complex throughout the unit?
  - How will students use critical, creative, and self-regulated thinking throughout the unit?
  - How much time will be devoted to each lesson/activity?
  - What kind of questions will you ask to see if students are understanding?

- **Step 7: Address the following questions about instructional strategies:**
  - What instructional strategies are most effective and efficient in teaching each lesson within the unit?
  - How will the learning environment support these strategies?
  - What is the teacher's role in each lesson?
  - What is the students' role in each lesson?

- **Step 8: Address the following questions about management:**
  - How and where will students work (classroom, field experiences, labs, groups, etc.)?
  - How will lessons be differentiated to accommodate for specific student readiness, interest, and learning profiles?
  - What additional resources will be needed in order to differentiate lessons?

Designing Units and Lessons
Coaching Tool (form continued)

Teachers

Name: _____

Dept/School: _____

Date: _____

- **Step 9: Address the following questions about materials and resources:**
  - How can technology support this unit?
  - What unusual (not commonly available) books, supplies, computer programs, videos, guest speakers, field trips, etc. will be needed?

- **Step 10: Address the following questions as a reflection at the end of the unit:**
  - Did all students master the concepts and skills?
  - What changes will be made the next time this unit is taught?

**Designing Units and Lessons
Coaching Tool** (form continued)

Teachers

Name: _____

Dept/School: _____

Date: _____

Template for Designing an Instructional Unit - Page 1

Step 1:

Content Knowledge:
What do you want your students to know?

Skills and Procedures:
What do you want your student to know how to do?

Step 2:

Standards and Benchmark Links:

Step 3:

Questions that will help students focus on the most important aspect of the unit:

Step 4:

Assessment:
Selected and Constructed Response

Products/Performances that Demonstrate Understanding

❐ Multiple Choice
❐ True/False
❐ Matching

❐ Fill-in-the-Blank
❐ Essay
❐ Short Answer
❐ Labeling
❐ Graph/Table
❐ Graphic Representation

❐ Service Project
❐ Movement
❐ Science Experiment
❐ Athletic Skill
❐ Demonstration
❐ Role Play
❐ Project
❐ Debate
❐ Model
❐ Presentation
❐ Musical Performance

❐ Portfolio
❐ Presentation Using Technology
❐ Research Paper
❐ Web Page
❐ Video

Source: Richard J. Stiggins, *Student-Involved Classroom Assessments*

Designing Units and Lessons
Coaching Tool (form continued)

Teachers

Name: _____

Dept/School: _____

Date: _____

Template for Designing an Instructional Unit - Page 2

Step 5:

Learning Connections:
What benchmarks can be connected?

Real World Connections:

Step 6:

Sequence of Learning Activities/Tasks:

1.

2.

3.

4.

5.

6.

7.

8.

9.

10.

Designing Units and Lessons
Coaching Tool (form continued)

Teachers

Name: _____

Dept/School: _____

Date: _____

Template for Designing an Instructional Unit - Page 3

Step 7:

Instructional Strategies:
Possible instructional strategies to use in the sequence of learning activities.

To Help Students Recall Information	To Help Students Comprehend Information	To Help Students Analyze Information	To Help Students Use Information
❏ Mindmapping ❏ Cornell Notetaking ❏ Mnemonics ❏ Concept Attainment ❏ Graphic Organizers ❏ Other	❏ Peer Editing ❏ Cooperative Learning Activities ❏ Discussion Webs ❏ Think-Pair-Share ❏ Goal Setting ❏ Reflection ❏ Other	❏ Writing-to-Learn Strategies ❏ Analogies ❏ Inductive Thinking Activities ❏ Making Patterns and Abstractions ❏ Error Analysis ❏ Simulations ❏ Other	❏ Decision Making ❏ Inventions ❏ Investigations ❏ Problem Solving ❏ Creative Thinking ❏ Experimental Inquiry ❏ Other

Step 8:

Encourage individual differences by incorporating various events, artifacts, content, and activities into lessons using Howard Gardner's *Multiple Intelligences*.

Verbal-Linguistic: *Books, stories, poetry, speeches*	Mathematical-Logical: *Puzzles, patterns, computers, graphs, predictions*	Musical: *Poems, songs, jingles, raps, chants*
Visual-Spatial: *Draw, manipulatives, storyboards, videos*	Bodily-Kinesthetic: *Role play, dramatize, games, dance, animations*	Interpersonal: *Discussions, interviews, cooperative games, teams*
Intrapersonal: *Reflections, record observations*	Naturalist: *Field trips, walks, outdoor activities*	Existential: *Community service, charity work*

Designing Units and Lessons
Coaching Tool (form continued)

Teachers

Name: _____

Dept/School: _____

Date: _____

Template for Designing an Instructional Unit - Page 4

Step 9:

Materials and resources:

Firsthand Experiences: *Field trips*	Visiting Experts:	Books/Readings:	DVD/Videos:
Computer Programs:	Internet Sites:	Music:	Other: *Simultations, magazines, posters, lab equipment, manipulatives, etc.*

Step 10:

Reflections after teaching the unit:

What did you learn about your students?

What did you learn about the content?

What did you learn about yourself?

What went well?

What were the surprises?

What would you do differently next time?

What do you need to learn more about?

**Designing Units and Lessons
Coaching Tool** (form continued)

Teachers

Name: _____

Dept/School: _____

Date: _____

FOLLOW-UP/REFLECTION:

How can you plan instruction to maximize learning for all students?

_____

_____

REFERENCES:

Danielson, C. (1996). *Teaching for understanding.* Alexandria, VA: ASCD.

Jacobs, H. H. (1989). *Interdisciplinary curriculum: Design and implementation.* Alexandria, VA: ASCD.

Jacobs, H. H. (1997). *Mapping the big picture: Integrating curriculum and assessment K-12.* Alexandria, VA: ASCD.

Tomlinson, C. A. (1996). *Differentiating instruction for mixed-ability classrooms.* Alexandria, VA: ASCD.

Wiggins, G., & McTighe, J. (1998). *Understanding by design.* Alexandria, VA: ASCD.

**Assessing Learning
Coaching Tool**

Teachers

Name: _____

Dept/School: _____

Date: _____

GOAL:

The teacher will develop an assessment plan that will include a variety of assessments. The assessments will address all of the instructional goals and reflect developmentally appropriate student participation.

DESCRIPTION:

Assessment methodologies must be appropriate to different types of instructional goals. Some goals can be assessed using selected or constructed responses. For more complex instructional goals, performance assessments are more appropriate. This type of assessment requires determining a scoring system or a rubric for evaluating students' authentic work.

HELPFUL SUGGESTIONS:

Tips for **selected response assessments.**
All selected response assessments should measure significant, not trivial details. The correct answer should require the specialized knowledge being tested, not common sense.

Multiple-Choice Tests:

- Test items consist of a stem followed by a correct answer and three or four distractors.
- Use familiar language in the stem and the possible answers.
- Test items should be stated in the positive.
- Responses should be about the same length.
- Avoid choices such as "all of the above"; "none of the above"; "only a & b."
- Arrange questions and options vertically rather than horizontally.

True/False Tests:

- Use simple, clear, precise language so there is no doubt about the correct answer.
- Avoid the use of specific determiners; for example, all, none, never, always, generally.
- Make use of popular misconceptions or beliefs as false statements.
- Randomize the sequence of true and false statements.
- Avoid negative statements, especially two negatives in one sentence.
- Have the student circle the word true or false rather than write T or F.

Matching Tests:

- Keep the stems and options on the same page.
- Place the shortest list on the right hand side of the page.
- Do not provide more than one answer for each stem.
- Put the options in some sort of logical order, e.g., alphabetical or numerical
- In the directions, indicate whether each response may be used once, more than once, or not at all.

Teachers

Name: _____

Dept/School: _____

Date: _____

Tips for **constructed response assessments.**

In response to a prompt, students construct an answer out of old and new knowledge. Since there is no one exact answer to these prompts, students are constructing new knowledge that likely differs slightly or significantly from that constructed by other students, thereby making scoring more challenging.

Essay Tests:

- Be sure that the directions and question asked are clear.
- Provide a space for the student to write his or her answer under the question.
- Provide a choice in essay questions that students can answer (three out of five).
- Make sure the questions can be answered satisfactorily in the allotted time.
- Be sure that the students know the meaning of the keywords—analyze, compare, contrast, criticize, describe, discuss, list, summarize, support, trace.
  - **Analyze**—break down the whole into parts.
  - **Compare**—bring out points of similarity and difference, with emphasis on similarities.
  - **Contrast**—stress the differences.
  - **Criticize**—point out the good and bad points of a situation or idea.
  - **Describe**—create a word picture in sequence or story form.
  - **Discuss**—examine an issue from all sides.
  - **List**—number or sequence the responses.
  - **Summarize**—present the main points in condensed form.
  - **Support**—to tell, in positive form, why a position or point of view is important.
  - **Trace**—present in step-by-step sequence a series of facts that are related in terms of time, order of importance, or cause/effect.

Tips for Scoring Essay Tests:

- Prepare some type of scoring guide, such as a rubric.
- Evaluate all of the students' responses to one question before proceeding to the next.
- Periodically rescore previously scored papers.
- Evaluate essays without knowing the identity of the writer.

Tips for **performance assessments.**

Performance assessments require the student to create performances or products that demonstrate his or her knowledge or skills. Performance tasks may include written or oral responses, presentations, demonstrations, investigations, etc.

Assessing Learning
Coaching Tool (form continued)

Teachers

Name: _____

Dept/School: _____

Date: _____

Developing Performance Assessments:

- Decide what the student should know and be able to do.
- Create a performance assessment task that is meaningful to the student and will engage the student in the task by connecting to real issues, problems, or themes.
- Decide on the product and performance the student will provide as evidence of understanding.
- Consider the extent of student choice for the product or performance.
    - Type of evidence?—written, performance, visual
    - Use of outside resources?
    - Individually/pairs/groups?
    - Audience?
    - Amount of time?
- Identify criteria for scoring the products or performance and the scoring tools that will be used. Present exemplars and scoring tools when the task is first assigned.

Chicago Public Schools has a Rubric Bank online with many excellent examples of rubrics created for performance assessments.
http://intranet.cps.k12.il.us/Assessments/Ideas_and_Rubrics/Rubric_Bank/rubric_bank.html

You can make your own rubrics or find ready-made rubrics at RubiStar. http://rubistar.4teachers.org/index.php

To engage students in the tasks, performance assessments should be written in a real life, meaningful context. Construct a scenario for a performance assessment, paying attention to what the student should know or be able to do.

Setting and Role *You have been asked to . . .*
Goal or Challenge *Your task is to . . .*
Product or Performance and Purpose *You will create or develop a . . .*
Audience *You will need to convince . . .*

Assessing Learning
Coaching Tool (form continued)

Teachers

Name: _____

Dept/School: _____

Date: _____

Designing Rubrics for Performance Assessments:

- Use action verbs to state the criteria in specific terms.
- Address expected learner outcomes.
- Describe what students are to know and do.
- Address the same criteria, in the same order at each level.
- Describe measurable qualities of a performance or product.
- Use helpful, understandable language.
- Use parallel language at each level.

Design a rubric for the performance assessment you have just created by creating the criteria for each level.

	Criteria 1	Criteria 2	Criteria 3	Criteria 4
4 **Excellent** (Excellence standard— exemplary performance or understanding)				
3 **Proficient** (Acceptable standard— solid performance or understanding)				
2 **Adequate** (Just meets acceptable standard—emerging or developing performance or understanding)				
1 **Limited** (Not yet meeting acceptable standard—serious errors, omissions, misconceptions)				

Teachers

Name: _____

Dept/School: _____

Date: _____

FOLLOW-UP/REFLECTION:

What three important ideas have you learned about performance assessment? What two questions or concerns do you still have about performance assessment? What is one step that you will take related to performance assessment?

_____

_____

REFERENCES:

Blum, R., & Arter, J. (1996). *A handbook for student performance assessment in an era of restructuring.* Alexandria, VA: ASCD.

Marzano, R. J., Pickering, D., & McTighe, J. (1993). *Assessing student outcomes: Performance assessment using the dimensions of learning model.* Alexandria, VA: ASCD.

McTighe, J. (1996). *Performance assessment in the classroom.* Sandy, UT: The Video Journal of Education.

Stiggins, R. J. (1996). *Assessment for quality learning: Program one and two.* The Video Journal of Education. Sandy, UT: The Video Journal of Education.

TEACHER PERFORMANCE
APPRAISAL COACHING TOOLS

TEACHERS

AREA 3: Managing Learning—Concerns the teacher engaging students in learning.

Indicators include:

- Communicating Verbally and Nonverbally
- Asking High-Quality Questions
- Facilitating Learning Experiences
- Giving Feedback
- Making Instructional Adjustments

**Communicating Verbally and Nonverbally
Coaching Tool**

Teachers

Name: _____

Dept/School: _____

Date: _____

GOAL:

The teacher will use spoken and written language that is clear, correct, and expressive. Well-chosen vocabulary will be used when giving directions and explaining procedures to students.

DESCRIPTION:

Directions give students their first impression of an activity. Well-constructed directions set a user-friendly tone for the entire activity.

HELPFUL SUGGESTIONS:

- Gain students' attention before giving directions.
- In order to make sure that students are giving their undivided attention, give the directions first and then present the materials to the students.
- Always accompany oral directions with written handouts or with an outline on the board, overhead, or a computer presentation tool. Be sensitive to both the auditory and the visual learner.
- Be clear and concise.
- Include words with exciting, active connotations whenever possible, so long as they do not obscure the meaning of the directions or procedures that are being given.
- Present oral instructions in small segments as students progress through the assignment rather than in one long barrage of instructions.
- Simplify directions as much as possible, eliminating needless words whenever possible.
- Think of different ways to reword directions.
- Model the directions by showing samples or by demonstrating.
- When writing a handout containing directions, distinguish successive tasks into separately numbered items.
- Properly sequence directions.
- Place general methods of operation and expectations on charts displayed around the room and on sheets to be included in student notebooks.
- Check for understanding by having students repeat the directions.

Communicating Verbally & Nonverbally
Coaching Tool (form continued)

Teachers

Name: _____

Dept/School: _____

Date: _____

Videotape or Audiotape Self-Review on Giving Effective Directions

	Very Satisfied	Satisfied	Needs Improvement	Not Applicable
1. Had students' attention before directions were presented.				
2. The directions were clear.				
3. The directions were concise.				
4. The directions were complete, including all crucial information needed for the activity.				
5. The directions were sequenced into component parts.				
6. Used modeling or demonstration when appropriate.				
7. Explained direction in more than one way.				
8. Stopped to check for student understanding.				
9. Obtained frequent student input and feedback.				
10. Presented directions with excitement in voice and in choice of words.				
11. Used illustrations with concrete or familiar references.				
12. Paused for breath.				

FOLLOW-UP/REFLECTION:

What are my strengths and weaknesses in giving verbal or written direction? How can I do a better job of giving students just enough guidance so they feel confident while leaving plenty of room for individual discovery?

_____

_____

REFERENCE:

Oliver, C., & Bowler, R. (1996). *Learning to learn.* New York: Simon & Schuster.

**Asking High-Quality Questions
Coaching Tool**

Teachers

Name: _____

Dept/School: _____

Date: _____

GOAL:

The teacher will use skilled, uniformly high-quality questioning to engage students in an exploration of content. Students have adequate time to respond to questions. Students formulate their own high-quality questions.

DESCRIPTION:

Higher-level questions are those requiring complex application (e.g., analysis, synthesis, and evaluation skills). Questions at higher levels of the taxonomy are usually most appropriate for encouraging students to think more deeply and critically, problem solving, encouraging discussions, and stimulating students to seek information on their own. Carefully framed questions enable students to reflect on their understanding and consider new possibilities.

HELPFUL SUGGESTIONS:

Types of Questions:

- **Factual: (F)**
  - Simple, straightforward, based on facts
  - *Naming, defining, identifying, giving yes/no responses*
  - Usually begin with: Who, What, When, Where . . .
  - Example: What are the parts of speech?

- **Convergent: (C)**
  - Represent the analysis or integration of given or remembered information
  - *Explaining, stating relationships, comparing, contrasting*
  - Usually begin with: Why, How, In what ways . . .
  - Example: In what ways does Michigan compare to New York?

- **Divergent: (D)**
  - Explore different avenues and create many variations and alternative answers
  - *Predicting, hypothesizing, inferring, or reconstructing*
  - Usually begin with: Imagine, Suppose, Predict, How might, If . . . then . . .
  - Example: Imagine what the world would be like without gravity!

- **Evaluative: (E)**
  - Deal with matters of judgment, value, and choice
  - *Judging, defending, justifying*
  - Usually begin with: Defend, Judge, Justify, What do you think about . . .
  - Example: What do you think about solar powered cars?

- **Combination: (CM)**
  - Blend of any combination from above
  - Example: Tell what character in the story was most ethical and justify your answer

- **Affective: (A)**
  - Questions that elicit expressions of attitude, values, or feelings
  - Example: How do you feel about that? Is that important to you?

Asking High-Quality Questions
Coaching Tool (form continued)

Teachers

Name: _____

Dept/School: _____

Date: _____

Steps and Suggestions for Planning Questions:

- Write the main questions in advance.
- Arrange questions in some logical sequence (specific to general, lower level to higher level, a sequence related to the content).
- Anticipate student responses. Consider the following: Will students have some typical misconceptions that might lead to incorrect answers? What type of response do I want from the students? Definition? Example? Solution? How will I handle incorrect responses?
- Phrase questions carefully.
- Ask questions that require an extended response, not just a "yes" or "no" unless a follow-up question will explore reasoning.
- Since students learn and study based on questions asked by the teacher, questions should be based on important rather than trivial content material.

Using Effective Communication Skills in the Classroom Environment:

- Students should feel free to ask questions of the instructor and their peers.
- Students should feel free to answer questions.
- Students should not feel threatened by giving an incorrect response.
- Eye contact should be made with the student answering the question.
- LISTEN to the student. The student should not be interrupted even if he or she is heading toward an incorrect answer.
- Make an attempt to randomly select students to respond to questions.
- Avoid letting some students dominate responding to questions being asked.
- Encourage students to answer difficult questions by providing cues or rephrasing.
- Probe for additional information if students' answers are incomplete or superficial.
- Paraphrase responses to check for understanding of responses that are not clear.
- Give students opportunities to ask questions.

Wait Time:

- Research indicates that students need at least three seconds to comprehend a question, consider the available information, formulate an answer, and begin to respond.
- Research indicates that the average classroom teacher allows less than one second of wait time.
- Lower-level questions require approximately three seconds of wait time.
- Higher-level questions may require wait time of five seconds or more.
- Complex higher-level questions need wait time, plus some time to note some ideas before responding.

Asking High-Quality Questions
Coaching Tool (form continued)

Teachers

Name: _____

Dept/School: _____

Date: _____

Designing a variety of types of questions.
Write a group of questions for a specific unit. Analyze them for the type of question.
F = Factual C = Convergent D = Divergent E = Evaluative CM = Combination A = Affective

Question	Question Type

**Videotape or Audiotape Self-Review of Types
of Questions Asked and Attending Behaviors to Student Responses**

	Very Satisfied	Satisfied	Needs Improvement	Not Applicable
1. Questions were appropriately phrased and understood by students.				
2. Questions were at the appropriate level for the content being taught.				
3. Questions followed a logical sequence.				
4. Questions required students to think at various levels of Bloom's Taxomony.				
5. Student responses were those that were anticipated.				
6. Students were encouraged to answer difficult, incomplete, or superficial questions.				
7. Called on students by name.				
8. Gave wait time after all questions to allow students time to think.				
9. Avoided interrupting students during responses.				
10. Checked for understanding of unclear responses by paraphrasing.				
11. Allowed and encouraged students to ask questions.				
12. Responded positively to student questions.				

Asking High-Quality Questions
Coaching Tool (form continued)

Teachers

Name: _____

Dept/School: _____

Date: _____

STUDENT SURVEY ON QUESTIONING

The following survey is designed to provide the teacher with information concerning students' perceptions of the questioning–interaction atmosphere in the classroom.

SURVEY ON QUESTIONING

Directions:

Respond to each statement below by placing a checkmark in the box that most closely matches how you feel about how your teacher asks questions and responds to answers during units of study.

	Usually	Sometimes	Seldom
1. I feel free to ask questions when I do not understand something in class.			
2. The questions presented to the class are not too difficult or too easy.			
3. The teacher asks questions to see if the students understand the presentation.			
4. The teacher misunderstands questions that the students ask.			
5. The teacher answers questions clearly and accurately.			
6. The teacher is patient and positive with students who ask questions.			
7. I feel comfortable responding to questions asked in class.			
8. The teacher asks challenging questions.			
9. The teacher asks open-ended questions.			
10. The teacher listens carefully to student responses to questions.			
11. The atmosphere in this classroom seems relaxed and friendly.			
12. Student participation is important in this classroom.			

Asking High-Quality Questions
Coaching Tool (form continued)

Teachers

Name: _____

Dept/School: _____

Date: _____

FOLLOW-UP/REFLECTION:

What are my strengths and weaknesses in developing and asking questions? How can I improve the interaction with my students when asking and responding to content questions?

_____

_____

REFERENCES:

Using "think-time" and "wait-time" skillfully in the classroom. (1994). Available at http://www.ed.gov/databases/ERIC_Digests/ed370885.html.

Johnson-Farris, N. (1990). *Questioning makes a difference.* Marion, IL: Pieces of Learning.

Johnson-Farris, N. (1996). *Active questioning: Questioning still makes a difference.* Marion, IL: Pieces of Learning.

Facilitating Learning Experiences
Coaching Tool

Teachers

Name: _____

Dept/School: _____

Date: _____

GOAL:

The teacher will design learning experiences that will engage students with content. These learning experiences will challenge students to construct deep understandings.

DESCRIPTION:

Challenging and engaging learning experiences are relevant, are authentic, and emphasize problem-based learning; permit student choice; encourage depth rather than breadth; and require students to think critically and creatively.

HELPFUL SUGGESTIONS:

When getting to know the content you are teaching, it is necessary to clarify the levels of thinking required to teach each standard. Will students need to recall information, relate to the content, connect the information to something else, or create something new and different with the new knowledge? Several "best practice" instructional strategies can be used to engage students effectively at each level of thinking. Some of these strategies are listed and defined below.

TO HELP STUDENTS RECALL INFORMATION:

Mindmapping—Mind Maps, developed by Tony Buzan, are an effective method of note-taking and useful for generating ideas by associations. To make a Mind Map, start in the center of the page with the main idea and work outward in all directions, producing a growing and organized structure composed of key words and key images. When complete, the Mind Map looks like a web. To aid visual memory, print the key words and use color, symbols, icons, 3D effects, arrows, and outlining.

Cornell Notetaking System—Developed by Walter Pauk (1989), the Cornell Notetaking System is a method for mastering information—not just recording facts. There are six steps.

Record (during lecture): write down facts and ideas in phrases, use abbreviations when possible (in the "details" column).

Reduce or question (after lecture): in your own words, write key words, phrases, or questions that serve as cues for notes taken in class (in the "main ideas" column).

Recite: with classroom notes covered, read each key word or question and recite the facts brought to mind.

Reflect and review: review your notes periodically.

Recapitulation (after lectures): summarize each main idea using complete sentences (in the "summary" section).

Main Ideas	Details
Summary:	

Facilitating Learning Experiences
Coaching Tool (form continued)

Teachers

Name: _____

Dept/School: _____

Date: _____

Mnemonic: A device, such as a formula or rhyme, used as an aid in remembering. Example: to remember the planets in order from the sun out to Pluto—My Very Educated Mother Just Served Us Nine Pizza pies. (My = Mercury, Very = Venus, Educated = Earth, Mother = Mars, Just = Jupiter, Served = Saturn, Us = Uranus, Nine = Neptune, Pizza pies = Pluto).

Concept Attainment: Students are presented with a mixed group of examples and non-examples of a concept. By observing these examples, students discuss and list the attributes of each until they develop a tentative hypothesis (definition) about the concept. This hypothesis is tested by applying it to other examples of the concept.

Graphic Organizer: Visual frameworks to help the learner make connections between concepts. Some forms of graphic organizers are used before learning and help remind the learners of what they already know about a subject. Other graphic organizers are designed to be used during learning to act as cues to what to look for in the structure of the resources or information. Still other graphic organizers are used during review activities and help to remind students of the number and variety of components they should be remembering. Generic examples are shown below. For additional examples, see:
http://www.writedesignonline.com/organizers/

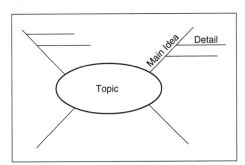

The Spider Map is used to describe a central idea: a thing, a process, a concept, a proposition. Helps to organize or brainstorm ideas.

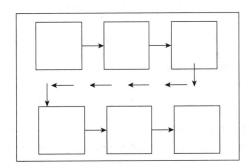

The Sequence Chain is used when prioritizing elements, a series of things or persons, or an orderly arrangement from first to last.

	Topic 1	Topic 2
Attribute 1		
Attribute 2		
Attribute 3		

The Compare and Contrast Matrix is used to compare and contrast shared and unique characteristics of two concepts, events, characters, people, or processes.

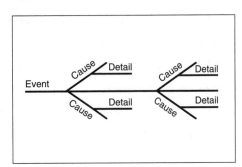

The Fishbone Map is used to help students determine the causal relationships in a complex idea or event.

**Facilitating Learning Experiences
Coaching Tool** (form continued)

Teachers

Name: _____

Dept/School: _____

Date: _____

TO HELP STUDENT COMPREHEND INFORMATION:

Peer Editing: Students read and give feedback on the work of their peers. A useful strategy to help students improve their analytical skills and also provides students with an alternative audience for their work.

Cooperative Learning Strategies: Students share knowledge with other students through a variety of structures. True cooperative learning includes five essential elements: positive interdependence, face-to-face interactions, individual accountability, social skills, and group processing skills.

- **Positive Interdependence:** Group members depends on each other to accomplish a shared goal or task.
- **Face-to-Face InteractionL:** Promoting success of group members by praising, encouraging, supporting, or assisting each other; students explain, discuss, and teach what they know to classmates.
- **Individual Accountability:** Each group member is held accountable for his or her work.
- **Social Skills:** Cooperative learning groups set the stage for students to learn social skills. Leadership, decision making, trust building, and communication are among the skills that are developed.
- **Group Processing:** Members of each cooperative learning group must discuss how well they are achieving their goals and maintaining effective working relationships.

Discussion Webs: A form of discussion that starts out with individual students formulating a response, then each student pairs with one other, and then the pairs pair to form groups of four. Finally, when the groups have refined their answers, they share their thoughts with the whole class.

Think-Pair-Share: Students think individually, then pair (discuss with partner), and then share ideas with class. This helps students to become more involved in group discussions.

Goal Setting: Steps to help students set goals:

1. Decide on a long-term goal. What do you want to accomplish?
2. Decide on a short-term goal that is based on the long-term goal.
3. Break the goal down into steps and develop an action plan.
4. Identify the obstacles and benefits of the goal.
5. List the resources and people that can help you reach your goal.
6. Keep a copy of the goal visible.
7. Take daily action toward the goal. Check things off that have been achieved.
8. Resolve not to quit until your goal has been reached.
9. Set a new goal and begin again.

Reflection: Students pause to think about and organize information gathered from reading, discussions, or other activities.

Facilitating Learning Experiences
Coaching Tool (form continued)

Teachers

Name: _____

Dept/School: _____

Date: _____

TO HELP STUDENT ANALYZE INFORMATION:

Writing to Learn: Help students realize the idea-generating potential of writing and its value by using the following writing-to-learn strategies.

- **Sentence Synthesis:** A quick-write strategy in which students construct meaningful sentences using three to four key words that capture the main ideas of a lesson or concept.

- **Question All-Write:** The teacher stops a lecture, class discussion, or video and asks students to respond to questions that check for understanding of the key concepts addressed.

- **Outcome Sentences:** The teacher provides prompts such as sentence stems (such as "I learned that, I wonder why") to invite student interaction with the content material.

- **Frames:** Skeletal paragraphs that contain information, important ideas, or transition words from the lesson. Students are expected to develop or extend the paragraphs.

- **Five Words: Three Words:** Students list five words that come to mind when they think of a topic. They get into pairs, trios, or groups of four to discuss why they selected these words and then select the three words they find most important to share with the whole class.

- **Sort Cards:** The teacher (and eventually students) generates descriptive words or phrases that describe key aspects of a topic, concept, or process. Students sort these words to sequence steps or refine descriptions. These sort cards can also be used for concept attainment using descriptors that do or do not apply to particular topics or processes.

- **Wordsplash:** Collections of key terms or concepts from passages that students are about to read or have read. Students are challenged to organize and use these words.

Analogies: Used to facilitate introducing concepts in ways that are concrete, meaningful, and relevant to the children. Teachers use analogies to help students form initial mental models of concepts (e.g., the human eye is like a camera, the heart is like a pump, and an electric circuit is like a water circuit).

The TWA (Teaching With Analogies) model (Glynn, Duit, & Thiele, 1995) provides guidelines for using analogies.

The basis of the TWA model consists of six operations that the teacher carries out when drawing an analogy:

1. Introduce target concept

2. Review analogy concept

3. Identify relevant features of target and analogy

4. Map similarities

5. Indicate where analogy breaks down

6. Draw conclusions

Facilitating Learning Experiences
Coaching Tool (form continued)

Teachers

Name: _____

Dept/School: _____

Date: _____

Inductive Reasoning: The process of inferring unknown generalizations or principles from information or observations. It is the process of making general conclusions from specific information or observations, sometimes referred to as reading between the lines. To learn more, see the Dimensions of Learning Model (Marzano & Pickering, 1997).

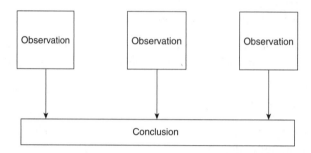

Abstracting: Finding and explaining general patterns in specific information or situations and then applying them to a new experience. To learn more, see the Dimensions of Learning Model (Marzano & Pickering, 1997).

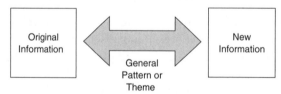

Error Analysis: The process of identifying and articulating errors in thinking. To learn more, see the Dimensions of Learning Model (Marzano & Pickering, 1997).

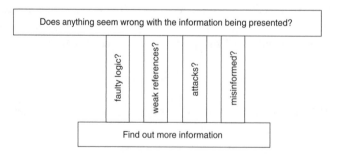

Simulations: Simulations are creative, complete units of instruction that incorporate traditionally taught material into a simulated environment in the classroom—anything from creating an advertising agency, to a trip across the ocean on a Spanish galleon or an English privateer, to establishing a space colony.

Students are organized into small groups and role-play either actual persons or characterizations of persons in history . . . or in social, economic, or political situations of today . . . or explorations of their place in the future. Goals are set for individuals, as well as for the groups with which they work.

Best place to purchase commercial simulations: http://www.interact-simulations.com/

Facilitating Learning Experiences
Coaching Tool (form continued)

Teachers

Name: _____

Dept/School: _____

Date: _____

TO HELP STUDENTS USE INFORMATION:

Decision Making: Students generate and apply criteria to select from among seemingly equal alternatives. To learn more, see the Dimensions of Learning Model (Marzano & Pickering, 1997).

Ideas	Criterion	Criterion	Criterion	Criterion	Tally
1.					
2.					
3.					

Inventions: Students create something to fill a need. An open-ended problem-solving task.

Investigations: Students do research and suggest or defend ways to clear up confusions about ideas or events. Three basic types are: Definitional (What are . . . ?), Historical (How . . . ? or Why . . . ?), and Projective (What if . . . ?). To learn more, see the Dimensions of Learning Model (Marzano & Pickering, 1997).

Problem-Based Learning: Students are involved in an inquiry process that resolves questions, curiosities, doubts, or uncertainties about something complex and might have multiple answers or solutions. Problem-based learning is a more student-directed curriculum. The following questions may help students organize information.

Problem-Based Learning Discussion Questions

What is the real problem we need to pinpoint?

What do we already know?

What do we not yet know?

What resources do we need to:

      Fully understand the problem?

      Begin to generate possible solutions?

How can we get the resources?

Who is doing what (team roles)?

What will be our criteria for solving the problem or evaluating our outcomes?

How can we divide and delegate tasks to team members?

How can we establish a time line for task completion with ongoing progress checks along the way?

When and how often do we meet for progress reports, problem solving, and accountability?

**Facilitating Learning Experiences
Coaching Tool** (form continued)

Teachers

Name: _____

Dept/School: _____

Date: _____

Experimental Design: Students develop and test explanations of things we observe.

What do you see or notice?
What hypothesis can you make about what you see or notice?
How can you test your hypothesis (make a prediction)?
Set up an experiment to test your prediction. 　Types of variables: 　　**Independent variable:** the only variable that is different from one experimental group to the next. It will determine the outcome of the experiment. It affects the dependent variable. 　　**Dependent variable:** the variable that is affected by the independent variable. This is what is measured in the experiment. 　　**Constants:** variables that must be kept exactly the same in all experimental groups so that only the independent variable is being tested.
Collect the data from your experiment (table or graph).
Analyze the data.
Draw conclusions.

FOLLOW-UP/REFLECTION:

How can you vary your instructional strategies to increase students' active participation in learning?

_____

_____

REFERENCES:

Glynn, S. M., Duit, R., & Thiele, R. B. (1995). Teaching science with analogies: A strategy for constructing knowledge. In S. M. Glynn and R. Duit (Eds.), *Learning science in the schools: Research reforming practice* (pp. 247-273). Mahwah, NJ: Erlbaum.

Marzano, R. J. (1992). *A different kind of classroom: Teaching with dimensions of learning.* Alexandria, VA: ASCD.

Marzano, R. J., & Pickering, D. J. (1997). *Dimensions of learning teacher's manual* (2nd ed.). Alexandria, VA: ASCD.

Wahlstrom, D. (1999). *Using data to improve student achievement.* Suffolk, VA: Successline Inc.

**Giving Feedback
Coaching Tool**

Teachers

Name: _____

Dept/School: _____

Date: _____

GOAL:

The teacher will provide students with regular, timely feedback on their performance to help students assess their progress.

DESCRIPTION:

Students receive a variety of different types of feedback from teachers on their performance. Some feedback is written and contains structured comments appropriate to the nature of the assignment or assessment. Some feedback may be nonverbal. Teachers convey meaning through facial expressions and gestures.

HELPFUL SUGGESTIONS:

- Feedback should be provided on all important work.
- The longer the delay between work and feedback, the less effective the feedback becomes. Ideally, feedback should be provided within minutes after finishing the task (and no longer than 24 hours after the task's completion) or immediately after a student asks or has answered a question.
- Feedback should explain to students what they have done *(clarify, inform, describe)*.
- Feedback should explain to students what they are doing correctly and incorrectly *(diagnose, differentiate, remediate)*.
- Feedback should help students move forward *(motivate, empower, liberate)*.
- The type of feedback will vary depending on whether the work is formative or summative.
- If the feedback is related to formative assessment, there needs to be a balance between positive and negative comments as well as strategies for improvement.
- There is evidence to suggest that students learn more from assessment experiences with good quality feedback.
- Students can effectively provide their own feedback or self-evaluation.
- Rubrics are a great way to provide students with feedback. Rubrics can be created on computers with templates available at Rubistar: http://rubistar.4teachers.org/

Giving Feedback
Coaching Tool (form continued)

Teachers

Name: _____

Dept/School: _____

Date: _____

Students can do meaningful reflection themselves if teachers provide them with regular time to think about their progress. At first, teachers may need to guide their reflection with questions such as these:

	Little or Nothing 1	A Fair Amount 2	A Great Deal 3
Overall, how much did you get out of today's class?			
What was the most important thing you learned?			
What have you done to contribute to your own success in this class?			
What is still unclear?			
What do you need help with?			
What single change by the teacher would have helped your learning?			
What changes do you need to make to improve your learning in this class?			
How much did you prepare for today's class?			
What one thing can you do to improve your preparation for class?			
How are you doing on the next assignment/project for this class?			
What one thing can the teacher do to help you make better progress on the assignment/project?			
What one thing can you do to help you make better progress on the assignment/project?			

FOLLOW-UP/REFLECTION:

Describe the type of feedback that you have given and its influence on your students. What type of feedback was not valuable or had a negative effect on students' work?

_____

_____

REFERENCES:

Marzano, R. J., Pickering, D. J., & Pollock, J. E. (2001). *Classroom instruction that works: Research-based strategies for increasing student achievement.* Alexandria, VA: Association of Supervision and Curriculum Development.

Ormrod, J. E. (2000). *Educational psychology: Developing learners* (3rd ed.). Upper Saddle River, NJ: Merrill.

Making Instructional Adjustments
Coaching Tool

Teachers

Name: _____

Dept/School: _____

Date: _____

GOAL:

The teacher will make adjustments to lessons if students are not learning successfully. The teacher will also enhance instruction based on students' questions or interests. The teacher is responsive to special needs students and draws upon a repertoire of strategies to meet student needs.

DESCRIPTION:

The teacher has the confidence, experience, and instructional repertoire to abandon a lesson and embark on a new direction. The teacher who is flexible and responsive taps into interests and other alternative approaches when a student is experiencing difficulty in learning.

HELPFUL SUGGESTIONS:

Survey Student Interests

- This can be done through an interest inventory, an interview or conference, or by asking students to respond to an open-ended questionnaire.
- Dr. Joseph Renzulli (1996) has developed an Interest-A-Lyzer for examining student interests. Susan Winebrenner (2000) also includes an interest survey in her book *Teaching Gifted Kids in the Regular Classroom*.

Have a Repertoire of Instructional Strategies

- Because "one size does not fit all," it is important that a variety of instructional strategies be used. Several different instructional strategies were mentioned in the "Engaging Students in Learning" coaching tool.

Use Flexible Grouping Strategies

- A teacher who is flexible and responsive uses flexible grouping strategies that employ several organizational patterns for instruction. Students are grouped and regrouped according to specific goals, activities, and individual needs. Most commonly, students are grouped by readiness level, learning profile, or interest.
- Many times, teachers lead groups in either whole-class or small group instruction. Other times, students work together in cooperative groups. Cooperative groups seem to be most effective when each member of the group is assigned a task and given a role. Roles should be rotated on a regular basis so that all students become proficient in each area.
    Roles could include:
        Facilitator: Keeps the group on task
        Recorder: Takes notes, writes summaries
        Reporter: Spokesperson for the group
        Materials Manager: Distributes and collects materials and work
        Timer: Keeps track of time, gives reminders
        Checker: Checks for accuracy in what the group is saying and writing

Making Instructional Adjustments
Coaching Tool (form continued)

Teachers

Name: _____

Dept/School: _____

Date: _____

FOLLOW-UP/REFLECTION:

How do you recognize when a lesson is falling apart and what do you do about it?

_____

_____

REFERENCES:

Renzulli, J. S. (1997). *Interest-A-Lyzer family of instruments: A manual for teachers.* Manfield Center, CT: Creative Learning Press.

Tomlinson, C. A. (1999). *The differentiated classroom: Responding to the needs of all learners.* Alexandria, VA: ASCD. Parts of this text are available in the ASCD Reading Room on the World Wide Web at http://www.ascd.org/readingroom/books/tomlin99toc.html

Winebrenner, S. (2000). *Teaching gifted kids in the regular classsroom* (rev. ed.). Minneapolis, MN: Free Spirit Publications.

Winebrenner, S. (2000). *Teaching kids with learning difficulties in the regular classroom: Strategies and techniques every teacher can use to challenge and motivate struggling students.* Minneapolis, MN: Free Spirit Publications.

TEACHER PERFORMANCE
APPRAISAL COACHING TOOLS

TEACHERS

AREA 4: Communicating—Concerns the teacher's professional responsibilities of keeping accurate information on students and communicating this information clearly and accurately.

Indicators include:

- Keeping Accurate Records
- Communicating With Families
- Serving and Advocating for Students

**Keeping Accurate Records
Coaching Tool**

Teachers

Name: _____

Dept/School: _____

Date: _____

GOAL:

The teacher will develop effective systems for maintaining information on student completion of assignments and for keeping track of student progress in learning. The teacher will also develop effective record keeping systems for noninstructional activities.

DESCRIPTION:

Teachers need well-designed systems for recording assignments that enable both teacher and students to easily and quickly know which assignments have been completed and which are still outstanding. Teachers also need to develop a record keeping system to keep track of which parts of the curriculum students have learned and which are still in progress. Checklists, records, and portfolios help to organize information about the student and will enable a teacher to provide this information to students' families. Record keeping can be accurately kept with paper and pencil, but computer technology makes record keeping easier and more accurate. Records must also be kept for noninstructional activities (lunch money, permission slips, etc.).

HELPFUL SUGGESTIONS:

- Develop a simple method of record keeping that can easily be kept up-to-date and is immediately available if parents or guardians wish to discuss their child's academic progress.
- Students can be taught to keep some of their own records using graphs or comments to show weekly progress.
- Keep an anecdotal file folder or three-ring binder with a divider for each student. The information kept here will help you discuss a student's progress professionally and efficiently.
  - Examples of information to keep in this folder or binder:
    - Biographical information—especially how to contact parents or guardians
    - Most recent progress report
    - Record of contacts made with parents or guardians
    - Blank paper to record notes about specific incidents
- Create a system for keeping track of papers for students who are absent. An "absent folder" could contain the necessary work the student will need when he or she returns to school.
- Use student portfolios to showcase students' best work. The work contained in student portfolios should be collected, selected, and reflected by the student so that the students' role in constructing understanding can be highlighted.

Keeping Accurate Records
Coaching Tool (form continued)

Teachers

Name: _____

Dept/School: _____

Date: _____

Students need to be taught to be responsible for collecting and selecting samples of their own work for their portfolio. The following evaluation tool could be included in student portfolios as the students reflect on the strengths and weakness of each piece contained in the portfolio.

Name: _____	PORTFOLIO ITEM REFLECTIONS		
Title of Item Selected	Strengths/Weaknesses	Improvements Needed	Teacher Comments
	Strengths:		
	Weaknesses:		
	Strengths:		
	Weaknesses:		
	Strengths:		
	Weaknesses:		
	Strengths:		
	Weaknesses:		

FOLLOW-UP/REFLECTION:

If using student portfolios, how will you store the portfolios in the classroom? What system will you use for reviewing and commenting on student work placed in the portfolio?

_____

_____

REFERENCE:

Student Portfolio Topic Pack. (2000-2001). ASCD Topic Pack. Alexandria, VA: ASCD.

Communicating With Families
Coaching Tool

Teachers

Name: _____

Dept/School: _____

Date: _____

GOAL:

The teacher will frequently communicate with parents or guardians about the instructional program. Information is communicated to parents or guardians on both positive and negative aspects of student progress and concerns are handled with sensitivity.

DESCRIPTION:

Effective communication keeps families informed of events in a class, such as announcements of upcoming events, reminders, schedules, procedures, standardized testing, grading systems, and behavioral standards. Many vehicles are useful for communication. Schools have formalized procedures for reporting to parents, but many teachers supplement these systems with additional information.

HELPFUL SUGGESTIONS:

Communicate:

- Call each parent or guardian to introduce yourself at the beginning of the year.
- During the year, call at least one parent each week to relay good news.
- Send a personal note.
- Create voice mail and e-mail systems that help parents contact teachers.
- Create a class Web site.
- Send a letter of introduction.
- Send frequent newsletter about school activities.
- Use languages with which parents feel comfortable.
- Make home visits.
- Send syllabus to parents that includes evaluation procedures, a tentative outline of the semester, homework policies, make-up procedures, how and when you can be reached, etc.

Welcome:

- Invite parents into the classroom
- Hold family learning events at school
- Attend school and community functions

Educate:

- Offer classes on special parenting topics on issues suggested from a parent survey

Involve:

- Ask parents to sign a contract
- Give family homework assignments

Help Parents to Contribute:

- Encourage volunteering
- Ask parents to share their expertise
- Chaperone field trips

Several of the ideas above were adapted from *Teachers' Best Ideas for Involving Parents*. The complete version of this booklet can be found on the PTA Members Only subscription Web site: http://www.pta. org/Subscr/subs1.asp.

Communicating With Families
Coaching Tool (form continued)

Teachers

Name: _____

Dept/School: _____

Date: _____

Telephone calls are an effective tool for maintaining good teacher/parent communication. Answering machines and cell phones make it easier than ever to reach parents. Use the following phone log to keep track of all calls made to parents—good news or bad news. A paper trail is very important for teachers today.

Date	Good/Bad News (+/−)	Parent's Correct name	Nature of Call	Response	Outcome

Communicating With Families
Coaching Tool (form continued)

Teachers

Name: _____

Dept/School: _____

Date: _____

FOLLOW-UP/REFLECTION:

Since parents and teachers share responsibility for creating a working relationship that fosters children's learning, it is important to establish a climate conducive to open communication. How can any parent–teacher differences that could arise be prevented or resolved?

_____

_____

REFERENCES:

Carpas, J., & Davis, K. B. (2002). *The elementary teacher's guide to parent and student communication.* Greensboro, NC: Carson Dellosa Publishing Company.

Developing Family/School Partnerships: Guidelines for Schools and School Districts. Fairfax, VA: National Coalition for Parent Involvement in Education.

No Child Left Behind—Parent Involvement. Available at http://www.ed.gov/legislation/ESEA02/pg2.html#sec1118

Tom, D., Mitchell, J., & Colen, K. (1995). *A note from your teacher: More than 450 ready-made notes for communication and personalizing report cards.* Teaching & Learning Co.

**Serving and Advocating for Students
Coaching Tool**

Teachers

Name: _____

Dept/School: _____

Date: _____

GOAL:

The teacher will be highly proactive in serving and advocating for students. The teacher will also make sure that all school-related decisions are based on the highest professional standards.

DESCRIPTION:

Professional teachers care deeply for the well-being of their students and step in on their behalf when needed. They are aware of, and alert to, the signs of child abuse. They are advocates for all students, particularly those who are traditionally underserved. Professional educators maintain an open mind and are willing to attempt new approaches to old problems. They strive to use the best data available to support action.

HELPFUL SUGGESTIONS:

Child Abuse

- What to do if you suspect child abuse:
  - Call your local police department if it is an emergency.
  - Call your state or local child abuse hotline.
  - Contact Childhelp USA, National Child Abuse Hotline @ 1-800-4-A-CHILD or at www. childhelpusa.org.
- Suspicion of child abuse is all that is needed to file a report.
- Information can be given anonymously.

Children With Disabilities

- The National Dissemination Center for Children With Disabilities (NICHCY) maintains a Web site that contains a wealth of information and resources related to the interest and concern to the well-being of children with disabilities. Here you will find information on:
  - Curriculum—Web sites, books, and articles on curriculum for students with disabilities
  - Disability Networks—where to find answers to questions regarding disabilities
  - Disability Publishers—a guide to curriculum, children's books, disability journals, educator materials, etc.
  - IEP—materials explaining the Individual Education Program (IEP)
  - U.S. Laws—learn about the top four U.S. education laws affecting children with disabilities
  - Many additional topics written in both English and Spanish
- Contact the National Dissemination Center for Children With Disabilites at:
  P.O. Box 1492
  Washington, DC 20013
  (800) 695-0285 · v/tty
  (202) 884-8441 · fax
  www.nichcy.org

Serving and Advocating for Students
Coaching Tool (form continued)

Teachers

Name: _____

Dept/School: _____

Date: _____

English as a Second Language (ESL) Students

- A comprehensive site for ESL, EFL, TOEIC, TOEFL, studying English, and learning English can be found at www.1-language.com.
- Another helpful resource for teachers is a monthly online journal: *The Internet TESL Journal for Teachers of English as a Second Language* (articles, research papers, lesson plans, classroom handouts, teaching ideas, and links). This journal can be found at http://iteslj.org

Go to the National Dissemenation Center for Children With Disabilities Web site at www.nichcy.org/states.htm to check for organizations and agencies in your state that would provide useful information for specific children with disabilities that are in your classroom. List the organizations and agencies as well as contact information that would target your needs.

Agency	Targeted Need	Contact Information	
		Phone	Web Address
Example: U.S. Department of Education	No Child Left Behind		http://www.ed.gov

FOLLOW-UP/REFLECTION:

What effect does the No Child Left Behind legislation have on your teaching approaches for children with disabilities, ESL students, etc.?

_____

_____

REFERENCES:

Childhelp USA: www.childhelpusa.org

National Dissemination Center for Children With Disabilities: www.nichcy.org

The Internet TESL Journal For Teachers of English as a Second Language: http://iteslj.org

TEACHER PERFORMANCE
APPRAISAL COACHING TOOLS

TEACHERS

AREA 5: Growing Professionally—Concerns the teacher's additional professional responsibilities for reflecting and self-evaluating on teaching to improve student learning, for keeping current with latest best practices, and for sharing new learning and action research with colleagues in the local school district or at the state and national levels.

Indicators include:

- Reflecting on Teaching
- Assuming Professional Leadership
- Developing Professionally

Teachers

**Reflecting on Teaching
Coaching Tool**

Name: _____

Dept/School: _____

Date: _____

GOAL:

The teacher will reflect on units and lessons by asking thoughtful questions and making accurate assessments of outcomes and then uses this information to make improvements.

DESCRIPTION:

As teachers reflect on units and lessons, the effectiveness and the extent to which goals were achieved are important to ponder. Teachers should be able to cite many specific examples from units and lessons and weigh the relative strengths and weaknesses of each. Drawing on an extensive repertoire of skills, teachers should decide upon specific alternative actions for future improvement of units and lessons.

HELPFUL SUGGESTIONS:

- Create a portfolio with specific examples from units and lessons, including samples of student work. "Creating a portfolio will help to provide a means for reflection; it offers the opportunity for critiquing one's work and evaluating the effectiveness of lessons or interpersonal interactions with students or peers" (Doolittle, 1994).
- Conduct action research. This is a process by which a teacher examines his or her own educational practice systematically and carefully using the techniques of research.
- Steps of action research include:
  a. Identify the question or problem.
  b. Develop an action plan to study this question or problem.
  c. Collect data directly related to the question or problem.
  d. Analyze the data (qualitative and quantitative).
  e. Share findings with colleagues and get feedback.
- Ask important questions about each step of the teaching/learning process. Use the following questions as a tool for reflection.

Questions to ask when reflecting on the unit plan:
1. Why am I teaching this unit?
2. Do I know the content of this unit well enough to teach it?
3. What do I need to learn in order to teach this unit effectively?
4. Does this unit address standards and benchmarks?
5. Do I have the materials and resources necessary to teach this unit?

Reflecting on Teaching
Coaching Tool (form continued)

Teachers

Name: _____

Dept/School: _____

Date: _____

Questions to ask when reflecting about students:

1. What do I want students to learn and be able to do?
2. What do my students already know about the content of this unit and how can I build upon this knowledge?
3. How can I build upon the students' interests?
4. Which students have special needs for which I need to accommodate?

Questions to ask about specific lessons:

1. What are the goals of this lesson?
2. What lesson sequence will work best?
3. How will I engage students in this lesson?
4. How much time will I devote to this lesson?
5. What questions will I ask during this lesson to make sure that students are understanding.
6. What materials, resources, and instructional strategies will I use for this lesson?
7. What difficulties might students experience? How do I plan to help students overcome these difficulties?
8. What do I picture my students and myself doing during this lesson?

Questions to ask about assessment:

1. How will I know what students are learning?
2. What different types of assessments will I use?
3. How will I keep track of student progress and how will I record this progress?
4. Will I design some type of culminating performance assessment?
5. How will the performance assessment be evaluated?

Questions to ask at the conclusion of the unit:

1. What were the strengths and weaknesses of the unit?
2. What key areas should I target for improvement and why?
3. Did the students learn what I intended?
4. What did I do that caused the unit to go well or not well?
5. What specific strategies helped the students to learn?
6. What was the most difficult thing about teaching this unit?
7. What did I learn about my students, the content, and myself as a teacher?

**Reflecting on Teaching
Coaching Tool** (form continued)

Teachers

Name: _____

Dept/School: _____

Date: _____

Use this tool as a checklist as data are collected as an information source for action research.

Quantitative (Hard) Data:	✓
Norm-referenced tests	
Criterion-referenced tests (Standards-based)	
Performance-based assessments	
Characteristics of school population:	
Ethnicity/race	
Mobility of students	
Free/reduced lunch program	
Qualitative (Soft) Data:	
Classroom grades	
Interviews/surveys with students, teachers, parents	
Attendance reports	
Discipline referrals	
Retention rates	
Positive behaviors	

FOLLOW-UP/REFLECTION:

How does reflection help you to critically analyze the teaching and learning that takes place in your classroom?

_____

_____

REFERENCE:

Doolittle, P. (1994). *Teacher portfolio assessment.* ERIC/AE Digest. Available at http://ericae.net/db/digs/ed385608.htm

**Assuming Professional Leadership
Coaching Tool**

Teachers

Name: _____

Dept/School: _____

Date: _____

GOAL:

The teacher will take initiative for assuming leadership in school and district projects. The teacher will also develop supportive and cooperative relationships with colleagues.

DESCRIPTION:

Professional educators share their expertise, materials, and insights with colleagues in order to work together to focus on the needs of students. Teacher leadership requires a considerable amount of time commitment. However, professional educators find this to be time well spent.

HELPFUL SUGGESTIONS:

Learn About Critical Friends Groups:

Critical friends groups consist of 4 to 10 teacher colleagues and administrators who agree to work together for the purpose of improving student achievement by looking closely at one another's practice and at student work.

An Example of a Dilemma That Might Be Brought to a Critical Friends Group:

You have given your students an opportunity to create a PowerPoint presentation about the causes and effects of the Civil War. You were pleased that the students were enthusiastic about the assignment and spent a great deal of time creating their presentations. However, when students presented their projects, you noticed that they were more concerned with the "bells and whistles" of the computer program than learning the critical lessons you had hoped for. You present the assignment, your rubric, and samples of your students' work to a critical friends group.

The Coalition for Essential Schools and the National School Reform Faculty provide training throughout the country for those interested in becoming critical friends group coaches.

> Coalition for Essential Schools
>
> http://www.essentialschools.org/
>
> National School Reform Faculty
>
> http://www.nsrfharmony.org/

Become a Mentor for a New Teacher:

Some of the topics that new teachers need to discuss include, but are not limited to the following: district personnel policy guidelines, curriculum guidelines, lesson planning, grading, professional development opportunities, state standards, technology, parent involvement, methods for dealing with a difficult parent, dealing with individual student differences, working with special needs students, classroom management, the school environment, where is everything, what resources are available, what are the procedures (written and unwritten rules), who's who, school myths and legends, greatest accomplishments and challenges, and the school's background.

Assuming Professional Leadership
Coaching Tool (form continued)

Teachers

Name: _____

Dept/School: _____

Date: _____

If you were to bring a dilemma about a specific class, about a particular aspect of a unit you taught, or about a certain student to a critical friends group, what would you share? Write a short account of a situation you find troubling or puzzling.

The situation:
What you did:
What the student(s) did:

FOLLOW-UP/REFLECTION:

Given adequate time and resources, what kind of leadership from teachers do you feel is most needed and why? What can be done to help more teachers step into leadership roles? Where would you like to take a leadership role?

_____

_____

REFERENCES:

Applyby, J. (1998). *Becoming critical friends: Reflections of an NSRF coach*. Providence: Annenberg Institute for School Reform.

Blythe, T., Allen, D., & Schieffelin Powell, B. (1999). *Looking together at student work: A companion guide to assessing student learning*. New York: Teachers College Press.

Marzano, R. J., Pickering, D. J., & Pollock, J. E. (2001). *Classroom instruction that works: Research based strategies for increasing student achievement*. Alexandria, VA: ASCD.

Nave, B. (2000). *Critical friends groups: Their impact on students, teachers, and schools*. Bloomington, IN: Annenberg Institute for School Reform.

Developing Professionally
Coaching Tool

Teachers

Name: _____

Dept/School: _____

Date: _____

GOAL:

The teacher seeks opportunities for professional development and initiates opportunities to make important contributions to the profession, such as mentoring new teachers or supervising student teachers, writing articles for publication, and making presentations.

DESCRIPTION:

Professional organizations and professional journals are important vehicles for informing educators. Attending regional, state, and national conferences and presenting classroom research is a valuable way to contribute to the profession.

HELPFUL SUGGESTIONS:

- As a professional educator it is important to keep the passion for teaching that drew you to the profession in the first place. In order to keep an open mind and be willing to attempt new approaches:
  - Read professional books, articles, and literature about your areas of interest
  - Attend professional development sessions and conferences
  - Keep a journal of your reflections and discoveries
  - Talk with teachers and others who have the passions for improving education
  - Take a graduate class at a local university
  - Do action research in your own classroom
- Examples of questions that could lead to an action research study:
  - Can popular literature be used to develop interest in science content?
  - How do we get parents interested in promoting literacy for their children?
  - How can students do a better job with self-evaluation?
  - Can technology promote literacy and reading?
  - Are we hurting students by encouraging them to use inventive spelling?

HELPFUL SUGGESTIONS
FOR MAKING A PRESENTATION:

1. Know Your Purpose and Your Time Limit

- Find out if you are to inform the audience of an issue, discuss a subject, or demonstrate a problem.
- The purpose determines the way you will approach the next steps.
- Know how much time you have to give the presentation and keep track of the time during the presentation.

2. Know Your Audience

- Find out who will be attending the presentation.
- Check to see if people are attending the presentation by choice of if it is compulsory.
- Consider the level of understanding the audience has on the topic.
- Contemplate what will they expect from you.
- Think over the educational jargon you will use and if your audience will understand it.

Teachers

Name: _____

Dept/School: _____

Date: _____

3. Research Your Topic Well

- Collect information from as many different types of sources as possible.
- Write notes on cards that are small, discreet, and easily handled in the palm of one hand.
- Color-code notes: opening, beginning, middle, conclusion.

4. Plan the Content and Structure

- Start—establish a relationship with the audience immediately.
- Opening—capture the interest of the audience.
- Introduction—include an outline of what you aim to cover in the presentation and the structure you will follow.
- Main Body—deliver the ideas clearly and logically, using visual and auditory examples.
- Conclusion—summarize the main points and make a final statement.
- Ask for questions.

5. Select Visual Aids

- Check the equipment to make sure that everything is working, especially if you are using computer-generated displays. Have a contingency plan in case the technology fails.
- Try out the visual aids in the room where you will be giving the presentation.
- If you use slides, pictures, or acetates on an overhead projector, make sure they are in order.
- If using an excerpt from a video, CD, or an audio tape, make sure it is cued up in advance.
- Keep visual aids simple and do not use too many. Visual aids should accompany the presentation, not dominate it.

6. Use Handouts

- Give handouts at the beginning of your presentation if you want to use them during your presentation and if you explain what they are for and how the audience will use them.
- Give handouts at the end of your presentation if they are a summary and you do not intend to use them during your presentation.

7. Be Aware of Verbal and Nonverbal Language

- Talk to the audience, not at them.
- Pay attention to the pace of your speech, tone and volume of your voice, and emphasis on words.
- Maintain eye contact with all members of the audience at various times.
- Be aware of your posture.
- Avoid nervous gestures and mannerisms.
- Smile at your audience in a friendly and approachable way.

Developing Professionally
Coaching Tool (form continued)

Teachers

Name: _____

Dept/School: _____

Date: _____

HELPFUL SUGGESTIONS FOR WRITING ARTICLES FOR PUBLICATION:

- Your experiences and ideas are valuable. Sharing them will help others with their practice.
- Most educations journals have specific guidelines for publication. Many journals seek manuscripts on particular topics or themes. Additional information on publication guidelines can be found on the Web sites of each professional organization or inside the front or back cover of the journal.
- If pictures of students are included in the article, a signed release is always required.
- Spellcheck the article and reread it at least three times. Have a proofreader read it as well.
- Use a standard computer software program. Most organizations accept Microsoft Word or Word Perfect. Use a laser printer for the work you submit. Avoid use of unusual type fonts or small type.
- Write a polite cover letter to the editor in which you also state that the article is not being simultaneously submitted to another journal and that it has not been previously published.
- If you receive a rejection slip, send your manuscript out again soon to another journal with some adjustments, especially if reasons were given for the rejection.

Use the following questions when submitting articles for publication on the results of action research.

What is the **title** for the article?
What was the **rationale** for doing the research?
What was found in the **review of the literature** on this topic?
What **question(s)** did you hope to answer as action research was conducted?
What is the **importance** of the project to you and your students and why?
What **methodology** was used?
- Who—populations/subjects
- What—materials/procedures
- How—type of data collection (examples: writing samples, anecdotal record, observations, audio/visual tapes, checklists, tests, surveys)

What did the **data analysis/findings** show (qualitative and quantitative)?
What are the practical **conclusions and implications** for the future?
What **references** were used?

Developing Professionally
Coaching Tool (form continued)

Teachers

Name: _____

Dept/School: _____

Date: _____

In this age of continuous improvement and increased accountability, it is important for professional educators to stay current on best practices and how to best meet the needs of all of the students we serve. Make it a goal to read; attend workshops, conferences, and classes; keep a journal; connect with other enthusiastic educators; and do research that will help to make a difference. Fill out the following chart and keep it handy so that you accomplish these goals.

TO BE COMPLETED WITHIN THE NEXT 12 MONTHS:			
Books/ Journals I Plan to Read	Workshops/ Conferences/Classes I Plan to Attend	People Who Can Help Me	Action Research Ideas

FOLLOW-UP/REFLECTION:

Make it a goal to present at a regional, state, or national conference or submit an article for publication. List below the conferences at which you would like to present and note the deadline for Calls for Proposals. Also, list journals to which you would consider submitting articles and note where to find the publication guidelines.

_____

_____

REFERENCES:

benShea, N. (2003). *Inspire, enlighten, & motivate: Great thoughts to enrich your next speech and you.* Thousand Oaks, CA: Corwin.

Jensen, E. (2000). *Trainer's bonanza: Over 1000 fabulous tips and tools.* San Diego, CA: The Brain Store.

CONCLUSION

The importance of principals knowing more than the basic teaching skills often included in brief summative tools cannot be overstated. Principals need to know not only what the following terms mean, but also how to implement them. Building community, designing learning, managing learning, communication, and growing professionally are key components to any successful school. They are the foundation for a successful school.

This chapter included coaching tools for teachers that were grounded in a teacher's work roles with all of its relevant responsibilities. They are sample templates that can be adapted to meet the unique needs of teachers as perceived by school leaders.

Chapter Four

Support Staff Performance Appraisal Coaching Tools

Like the teacher performance appraisal, the support staff appraisal should be based on the assumption that the staff member is a qualified, capable asset to be developed. The overall goal of this process is to continually remind support staff of the specific job responsibilities and skills of his or her unique position, self-evaluate based on reflecting how his or her performance measures up to the expectations of his or her job, and set goals for improvement.

What is different about support staff performance appraisals is that they are seldom implemented in any form other than a checklist, if that. Support staff is often caught between the central office of the school district and the building principal, and sometimes staff members are never evaluated at all, unless there is a problem with their performance. When that happens, then the performance appraisal process becomes punitive and not developmental.

Ultimately, the overriding purpose of all support staff personnel is to facilitate the educational staff members' ability to do their jobs. They should make the teacher's and administrator's job "doable," by eliminating problems unrelated to teaching and learning. For example, the school nurse or secretary can initially handle a student's need to call home in case of illness. The school custodian can make certain that the cafeteria is cleaned well after lunch in time for an instructional assembly and that each room is cleaned and prepared for the students and teachers the following day. The school bus driver can establish rules for his or her bus that reflect the school district's policy, and he or she can enforce the rules before the administrator needs to be consulted. In addition to their own specific and unique job responsibilities, all support staff members should consistently demonstrate flexibility, excellent communication skills and conflict management skills, and the ability to work with people from all cultural and socioeconomic backgrounds.

Moreover, support staff members need to grow professionally each year. Unfortunately, this population of school employees has historically been neglected when it comes to training for improvement. School districts are reluctant to spend any resources on support staff development, except to help them learn new technology to perform specific tasks that are unique to their jobs. They rarely have the opportunity to learn any new information in the areas of interpersonal skills (i.e., conflict management), personal management skills (i.e., stress/time management), or thinking skills (i.e., problem solving). Through a school district's commitment to all stakeholders' improved performance using similar appraisal formats, this current attitude and behavior toward support staff should change.

Also a key point to remember is that the responsibility for improved performance is shared by both the support staff member and his or her supervisor. Therefore, the supervisor must be familiar with the job expectations and competencies that are assigned to each support staff member before he or she can assume responsibility for implementing an effective performance appraisal process for the employee. For example, in the case of a principal, he or she may need a general training by the human resource department on what specific expectations and competencies exist for each support staff position in his or her building.

The instruments developed here encourage both human and material resources to improve performance and will provide a written record for the assessment and improvement of performance on six general areas of responsibility:

- Communication
- Conflict Management
- Public Relations
- Stress Management
- Team Building
- Time Management

Support Staff

Communication Skills Introduction

Name: _____

Dept/School: _____

Date: _____

INTRODUCTION TO COMMUNICATION SKILLS

To understand how to communicate better, you need to first understand what good communication implies. *Communication is not what you say; it's what they hear and what they think you meant.* Communication is your listener's perception and understanding. Good communication, therefore, occurs when your intent equals their perception.

How do you communicate? Research says that 93% of communication is nonverbal. Therefore, it is necessary for you to learn how to use nonverbal skills, the first major part of successful communication, effectively. What are some nonverbal signals, and how do you recognize them?

- **Time:** Keeping someone waiting for a meeting or by making a meeting or appointment shorter than it should be.
- **Furniture Arrangements:** Using furniture as barriers between people or by setting them against the wall.
- **Attractiveness:** Creating feelings in people through the surroundings that carry over to your communication.
- **Proximity:** Moving away from the person exaggerates differences; being close to a person shows a warm, positive attitude. However, be careful not to intrude on another person's "personal space."
- **Posture:** Conveying energy, fatigue, interest, boredom, approval, disgust, anxiety, confidence, like, dislike, and approachability through the way you carry yourself.
- **Gestures:** Usually moving hands and head frequently, as well as keeping hands in a relaxed, open-palmed position are generally seen as positive signals. Infrequent gestures send negative signals, as do clenched fists or other threatening movements.
- **Facial Expressions:** Gesturing with your head and face are probably the clearest indicators of interpersonal attitudes. Nodding the head is positive. Shaking it from side to side is negative. Lowering the head, or peering over eyeglasses usually indicates skepticism or suspicion. **Eye contact is the key nonverbal indicator**. It indicates a desire for communication or feedback and friendliness. Lack of eye contact may indicate either dislike or lack of interest in western cultures.
- **Hands and Feet:** Beating the floor constantly with your feet indicates tension and anxiety. Frequently shifting your legs from one knee to the other may reveal restlessness.
- **Silence:** Timing of a pause or a prolonged silence can convey powerful emotions or it can demonstrate interest and show genuine concern and encourage conversation.
- **Voice Characteristics:** Speaking loud and rapidly, or at a high pitch, can indicate anger.

Support Staff

Communication Skills Introduction
(form continued)

Name: _____

Dept/School: _____

Date: _____

Now, you cannot control how effectively others interpret your nonverbal cues. But you do have control over how effectively you send the message—either orally or in writing. To improve your oral communication skills, the second part of effective communication, remember these approaches:

- *Keep it simple.*
- *Avoid "crutch" words like "basically," "honestly," "you know," etc.*
- *Be positive versus negative.*
- *Talk the person's language; people need to feel valued.*
- *Never assume what people should know.*

The third major part of successful communication is being a good listener. Most people listen to only 25% of what they actually hear. The other 75% is tuned out. Successful listening requires active listening:

- Try to understand what the sender is feeling or what his or her message means.
- Paraphrase what you understand was said.
- Do not send messages of your own (advice, evaluations, or questions). Give feedback only on what you thought the sender's message meant.

There are six essential steps to improve your listening skills:

1. Let the speaker finish what he or she is saying before you respond.
2. Concentrate on what the speaker is saying.
3. Try to eliminate outside distractions during the conversation.
4. Study the speaker's tone, as well as what was said.
5. Pace your responses with those of the speaker, repeating the words he or she uses.
6. Paraphrase what the speaker said to make sure that you understood the meaning of his or her message.

Finally, the fourth component of effective communication is conflict communication. When dealing with angry people, try not to return aggression for aggression. Empathize, while paraphrasing and acknowledging their feelings, and let people vent. If they talk long enough, they may even hear a solution in their own words! Last but certainly not least, don't take people's anger personally! They are angry at the situation, and you are the first representative of the organization to whom they can directly state their feelings. Try to have an open posture, lean slightly forward toward them, maintain eye contact, and nod to let them see that you are truly listening and that you understand their frustration. You will be surprised at how quickly this approach will deflate their anger and enable them to be more rational very quickly.

If you practice all of these approaches, your communication skills will improve greatly!

Support Staff

**Communication Skills
Coaching Tool** (form continued)

Name: _____

Dept/School: _____

Date: _____

COMMUNICATION SKILLS SELF-ANALYSIS

Listening Skills:

1. **I listen to the feeling and emotions that are expressed by co-workers, staff, and students.**
    a. Rarely
    b. Sometimes
    c. Most of the time

2. **I let the speaker finish what he or she is saying before I respond.**
    a. Rarely
    b. Sometimes
    c. Most of the time

3. **I paraphrase what the speaker said to make sure I heard it properly and understand the meaning of his or her message.**
    a. Rarely
    b. Sometimes
    c. Most of the time

4. **In a conversation, I am comfortable with periods of silence.**
    a. Rarely
    b. Sometimes
    c. Most of the time

5. **When I don't understand a question, I ask for more explanation.**
    a. Rarely
    b. Sometimes
    c. Most of the time

6. **I find it easy to see things from someone else's viewpoint.**
    a. Rarely
    b. Sometimes
    c. Most of the time

7. **I notice the mood of others by looking at them while we are conversing.**
    a. Rarely
    b. Sometimes
    c. Most of the time

8. **I get so involved in what I have to say that I am unaware of the reactions of my listeners.**
    a. Rarely
    b. Sometimes
    c. Most of the time

9. **I listen attentively to people's ideas and concerns.**
    a. Rarely
    b. Sometimes
    c. Most of the time

10. **I usually try to understand the interests and important concerns of others.**
    a. Rarely
    b. Sometimes
    c. Most of the time

Support Staff

**Communication Skills
Coaching Tool** (form continued)

Name: _____

Dept/School: _____

Date: _____

Oral Communication Skills:

1. **I plan my communications with others to accomplish my goals.**
   a. Rarely
   b. Sometimes
   c. Most of the time

2. **I try to speak in a positive manner.**
   a. Rarely
   b. Sometimes
   c. Most of the time

3. **I manage to explain my ideas clearly.**
   a. Rarely
   b. Sometimes
   c. Most of the time

4. **I do not find it hard to express my feelings.**
   a. Rarely
   b. Sometimes
   c. Most of the time

5. **I do not raise my voice when I am frustrated.**
   a. Rarely
   b. Sometimes
   c. Most of the time

6. **I do not tend to dominate a conversation.**
   a. Rarely
   b. Sometimes
   c. Most of the time

7. **I do not find it hard to express my opinions when others don't share them.**
   a. Rarely
   b. Sometimes
   c. Most of the time

8. **I don't assume that what is important to me is important to everyone.**
   a. Rarely
   b. Sometimes
   c. Most of the time

9. **I consistently refer to the 5 questions that will help make my communication more effective:**
   1. **What?**   What is the message I am trying to communicate?
   2. **Where?**   Where will the communication occur?
   3. **Why?**   What do I want accomplished in my conversation?
   4. **Who?**   With whom am I interacting?
   5. **How?**   How will I communicate my message?
   a. Rarely
   b. Sometimes
   c. Most of the time

10. **I let the other person know that I care about what he or she is saying.**
    a. Rarely
    b. Sometimes
    c. Most of the time

Support Staff

**Communication Skills
Coaching Tool** (form continued)

Name: _____

Dept/School: _____

Date: _____

Conflict Communication Skills:

1. **When someone attacks me verbally, I tend to not take it personally.**
   a. Rarely
   b. Sometimes
   c. Most of the time

2. **I am able to accurately interpret what others are feeling, based on their choice of words, tone of voice, expressions, and other nonverbal behavior.**
   a. Rarely
   b. Sometimes
   c. Most of the time

3. **I try to find nonthreatening ways to approach others about sensitive issues.**
   a. Rarely
   b. Sometimes
   c. Most of the time

4. **I am able to resolve problems without losing control of my emotions.**
   a. Rarely
   b. Sometimes
   c. Most of the time

5. **When I am not directly responsible for a hostile person's problem, I apologize and do my best to solve the problem.**
   a. Rarely
   b. Sometimes
   c. Most of the time

6. **I try to maintain eye contact with the hostile person while he or she is venting.**
   a. Rarely
   b. Sometimes
   c. Most of the time

7. **When someone is hostile toward me, I try to reflect his or her feelings, restate his or her concerns, and resolve the problem.**
   a. Rarely
   b. Sometimes
   c. Most of the time

8. **In hostile situations I try to present arguments that address others' most important concerns and result in a win–win solution.**
   a. Rarely
   b. Sometimes
   c. Most of the time

9. **When I am verbally attacked, I try to negotiate.**
   a. Rarely
   b. Sometimes
   c. Most of the time

10. **I know that if I ever sense danger, that I should leave the area immediately and consult my supervisor.**
    a. Rarely
    b. Sometimes
    c. Most of the time

Support Staff

Communication Skills
Coaching Tool (form continued)

Name: _____

Dept/School: _____

Date: _____

11. **I am aware of my organization's policies regarding hostile situations, and I talk to my supervisor about any specific situations that apply to my workplace.**
    a. Rarely
    b. Sometimes
    c. Most of the time

12. **When I think that I might have hurt someone, I apologize.**
    a. Rarely
    b. Sometimes
    c. Most of the time

13. **I do not become defensive when I am criticized.**
    a. Rarely
    b. Sometimes
    c. Most of the time

14. **When I am angry, I admit it.**
    a. Rarely
    b. Sometimes
    c. Most of the time

15. **I do not tend to jump to conclusions.**
    a. Rarely
    b. Sometimes
    c. Most of the time

16. **I do not tend to delay discussing touchy topics.**
    a. Rarely
    b. Sometimes
    c. Most of the time

17. **I am able to address someone who has hurt my feelings.**
    a. Rarely
    b. Sometimes
    c. Most of the time

18. **I do not avoid addressing my differences with people, because they might get angry with me.**
    a. Rarely
    b. Sometimes
    c. Most of the time

19. **I do not get upset if someone disagrees with me, especially if that individual does not have my experience.**
    a. Rarely
    b. Sometimes
    c. Most of the time

20. **I am able to receive negative feedback without getting defensive.**
    a. Rarely
    b. Sometimes
    c. Most of the time

Support Staff

**Communication Skills
Coaching Tool** (form continued)

Name: _____

Dept/School: _____

Date: _____

Nonverbal Communication Skills:

Nonverbal communication skills is the process of sending and receiving wordless messages through hand gestures, eye contact, facial expressions, body posture, tone of voice, use of humor, and body positioning in space. Nonverbal cues include all of the signs used by individuals to express themselves outside of speech and manual sign language.

Successful people are able to understand nonverbal signals and use them to their advantage. They can adapt their presentation to the unspoken "messages" they pick up. For example, when people are getting along with one another, they face each other directly, and they lean in toward one another while maintaining eye contact.

1. **I understand that it's not only what I say but how I say it that is important in my communication.**
   a. Rarely
   b. Sometimes
   c. Most of the time

2. **I am consistently aware of nonverbal behavior in my workplace, and I try to adapt my behavior to my perception of how the other person is feeling or what he or she is thinking.**
   a. Rarely
   b. Sometimes
   c. Most of the time

3. **I consistently try to maintain eye contact with the person with whom I am speaking.**
   a. Rarely
   b. Sometimes
   c. Most of the time

4. **I try to convey interest, concern, warmth, and credibility in my nonverbal behavior.**
   a. Rarely
   b. Sometimes
   c. Most of the time

5. **I try to smile at people most of the time, as I know that projects my happiness, my friendliness, my warmth, my openness, and approachability.**
   a. Rarely
   b. Sometimes
   c. Most of the time

6. **I try to use a lot of gestures when I'm speaking, as I feel it makes my messages more interesting and enjoyable.**
   a. Rarely
   b. Sometimes
   c. Most of the time

7. **I frequently nod my head to reassure someone who is sharing an idea or confidence with me.**
   a. Rarely
   b. Sometimes
   c. Most of the time

8. **I am aware of my body posture at all times. When I stand, I try to straighten my back without appearing rigid. When I sit, I lean a little forward toward the person to whom I am talking to show interest and that I am approachable.**
   a. Rarely
   b. Sometimes
   c. Most of the time

Support Staff

Communication Skills
Coaching Tool (form continued)

Name: _____

Dept/School: _____

Date: _____

9. **I am constantly aware of the tone, pitch, rhythm, inflection and loudness of my voice when I am speaking.**
   a. Rarely
   b. Sometimes
   c. Most of the time

10. **I often use humor to relieve stress, and I am able to laugh at myself easily. This makes the workplace more fun and encourages others to not take themselves too seriously!**
    a. Rarely
    b. Sometimes
    c. Most of the time

Support Staff

**Communication Skills
Coaching Tool** (form continued)

Name: _____

Dept/School: _____

Date: _____

SCORING SHEET

A = 1 point
B = 2 points
C = 3 points

LISTENING SKILLS:

Most of the Time:	30-26 points
Sometimes:	25-21 points
Rarely:	20 points and below

Most of the Time:

Your listening ability is excellent. You listen for information and empathize with the speaker to let him or her know that you care. You organize and make sense of the information, and effectively paraphrase the speaker's message. You're able to eliminate distractions, and you can make effective decisions based on the information provided.

Sometimes:

You have some difficulty paying attention or finding interest in what the speaker is saying. You do not stay actively involved in the conversation by asking questions, and sometimes you interrupt by offering your own opinion without fully understanding the speaker's message.

Rarely:

You're an inattentive listener. You rarely keep an open mind while listening to others, and you often interrupt other speakers to get your own point across. You may be too aggressive with your criticism, or you may be too afraid to voice your true feelings. You are unable to accurately paraphrase the speaker's message, as you're unable to make connections between your own life and the topic.

ORAL COMMUNICATION SKILLS:

Most of the Time:	30-26 points
Sometimes:	25-21 points
Rarely:	20 points and below

Most of the Time:

You have an excellent ability to get your point across to others clearly and effectively. You check for understanding; you are empathetic in your conversation, you use "I" statements that define how you feel rather than go after the individual when you give criticism, you are able to sense how others are feeling by "reading" their nonverbal behavior, and you are able to express differing opinions and stand up for yourself without losing control of your emotions.

Sometimes:

You seem to have a basic understanding of what it takes to deliver a message effectively, although you occasionally have difficulty putting that knowledge into action. Check for understanding more frequently, and try to put yourself in your listener's shoes to see if there is a better way to get your idea across. You are sensitive to others' feelings, though you could improve on reading people's nonverbal body language. You are not completely proficient in your ability to manage your emotional responses, and sometimes you avoid discussing sensitive issues. You are occasionally reluctant to express different opinions and stand up for yourself.

Rarely:

You have difficulty delivering a succinct message, and you rarely if ever check for understanding. You are oblivious to others' feelings, and are generally unaware of their nonverbal communication. You are unable to express your emotions calmly, and you often criticize others harshly when they have difficulty understanding your message.

Support Staff

**Communication Skills
Coaching Tool** (form continued)

Name: _____

Dept/School: _____

Date: _____

CONFLICT COMMUNICATION SKILLS:

Most of the Time: 60-52 points
Sometimes: 51-42 points
Rarely: 41 points and below

Most of the Time:

You are excellent at managing the emotional part of the communication process. You are completely comfortable expressing your feelings or getting involved in potentially charged situations. You are aware of other peoples' sensitivities and deal with their feelings in a productive manner. You use "I" statements to deliver criticism, and you don't avoid the discussion of sensitive issues. You stand up for yourself without losing your empathy for the listener. You read nonverbal behavior well, and use this information when deciding how to approach a potential conflict situation.

Sometimes:

You are slightly reserved when expressing yourself in emotionally charged situations. Although you can be good at reading other people's body language, sometimes you lose control of your emotions and forget to use that information! You occasionally hesitate to express yourself, as you want to avoid sensitive issues.

Rarely:

You have little or no control over your own emotions. You criticize an individual, rather than his or her ideas, and your intimidation and lack of empathy challenges your listeners to challenge you! You are insensitive to other people's feelings and are unable to read nonverbal behavior.

NONVERBAL COMMUNICATION SKILLS:

Most of the Time: 30-26 points
Sometimes: 25-21 points
Rarely: 20 points and below

Most of the Time:

You use all of the nonverbal behaviors frequently and effectively. Your eye contact is direct without being threatening; you use warm facial expressions and humor to put people at ease; you are aware of your proximity to others and do not invade their personal space; and you consistently use a soft, consistent tone of voice and rhythm when you speak.

Sometimes:

You use some nonverbal behaviors consistently, but you avoid others such as maintaining eye contact and smiling at people whom you do not know. You need to identify your strong and weak skills and make a conscious effort to improve those skill areas.

Rarely:

You are uncomfortable using nonverbal behaviors. You rarely smile, use humor, lean toward the person with whom you are speaking, maintain eye contact, or vary your tone of voice. You appear to be bored, distant, and not much fun.

Support Staff

Communication Skills
Coaching Tool (form continued)

Name: _____

Dept/School: _____

Date: _____

Individual Development Plan for
Communication Skills
Select 2–3 goals

Problem to be Improved	Strategies	Date to be Completed
1.		
2.		
3.		

COMMUNICATION SKILLS REFERENCES

Beach, D. M., & Reinhartz, J. (2000). *Supervisory leadership: Focus on instruction.*

Bolton, R. (1986). *People skills.* Englewood Cliffs, NJ: Prentice Hall.

Bolton, R., & Grover, D. (1996). *People styles at work.* New York: Amacom Books.

Booker, D. (1994). *Communicate with confidence!* New York: McGraw Hill Trade.

Burley-Allen, M. (1995). *Listening: The forgotten skill: A self-teaching guide.* (2nd ed.). New York: John Wiley and Sons.

Communication Briefings. (1987). *The best ideas in employee communication.* Alexandria, VA: Author.

Condrill, J., & Bough, B. (1998). *101 ways to improve your communications skills instantly.* New York: McGraw Hill.

Covey, S. (1990). *The seven habits of highly effective people.* Provo, UT: Institute for Principle-Centered Leadership.

Daniels-Booker, D. (1994). *Communicate with confidence: How to say it right the first and every time.* New York: McGraw Hill.

DuFour, R., & Eaker, R. (1998). *Professional learning communities at work: Best practices for enhancing student achievement.* Bloomington, IN: National Education Service.

Eales-White, R. (1998). *Ask the right question: How to get what you want every time and in every situation.* New York: McGraw Hill.

Fairfield Poley, M. (1995). *Mastering the art of communication: Your keys to developing a more effective personal style.* Boulder, CO: Skillpath Publications-Career Track Publishers.

Harris, R., & Addison, F. (1993). *Open-ended questioning: A handbook for educators.* New York: Pearson Education-Wesley.

Heim, P. (1996). *Invisible rules: Men, women, and teams.* New Zealand: Cynosure Productions.

Krisco, K. (1997). *Leadership and the art of communication.* New York: Prima Publications, Random House.

Leeds, D. (1995). *Smart questions.* Berkeley, CA.: Berkeley Publishing Groups.

Robbins, H. (1992). *How to speak and listen effectively.* New York: American Management Association.

Stettner, M. (1995). *The art of winning conversation.* Englewood Cliffs, NJ: Prentice Hall.

Swets, P. (1986). *The art of talking so people will listen.* Englewood Cliffs, NJ: Prentice Hall.

Walton, D. (1989). *Are you communicating?* New York: McGraw Hill.

Support Staff

Conflict Management Introduction

Name: _____

Dept/School: _____

Date: _____

INTRODUCTION TO CONFLICT MANAGEMENT

Conflicts arise out of a lack of an individual's basic human needs not being met. What are common human needs?

- To feel welcomed
- To be understood
- To feel comfortable
- To receive help or assistance
- To feel important
- To be recognized
- To be respected

If any of these are threatened or questioned, people react. Therefore, more often than not, it is easier for us to adopt our behavior to the situation and to the individual than to change the difficult person's behavior or attitude. The key is to try to understand why people behave in particular ways.

In communicating with others, it is always important to keep the basic human needs in mind. We need to understand why we think it is difficult to work with some people and not with others. Quite often the reason lies within our own approach and reaction to different personalities. It is important to understand social styles and how they respond differently to conflict. For example, those with an aggressive personality may thrive on conflict; those who are by nature collaborative may avoid it whenever possible. Conflict of issues is healthy; conflict of personalities is not.

You need to be able to understand your own style and tendencies for dealing with conflict. Then you need to understand your audience as well. Once you have this information, you'll be able to select the appropriate behavior for particular situations. We tend to act more favorably to people who are similar to us. For us to interact with different kinds of people, we need to informally determine what general style that person is and how to get along with that individual without facing too many obstacles. We also need to have an understanding of what kind of people we are, so that we know how we will have to adapt to improve working relationships. Keeping an open mind and communication are the key elements in dealing effectively with others.

Finally, focus on the importance of building long-term relationships, partnerships, and teamwork with internal and external customers. It is important to resolve conflict in a win–win manner and to do it in a way that sustains positive social interaction.

Support Staff

**Conflict Management
Coaching Tool**

Name: _____

Dept/School: _____

Date: _____

Self-Appraisal:

1. **When I am confronted with a specific boss, colleague, or subordinate who's making my life miserable, I am able to take action to improve my situation.**
   a. Rarely
   b. Sometimes
   c. Most of the time

2. **I would rather deal with a difficult person than try to "get even" with him or her again.**
   a. Rarely
   b. Sometimes
   c. Most of the time

3. **I am able to put problem people in perspective and not let them control my behavior.**
   a. Rarely
   b. Sometimes
   c. Most of the time

4. **I am able to vent my frustrations with difficult people, if I can get away from them for a while and then think about what really is important to me in my work life.**
   a. Rarely
   b. Sometimes
   c. Most of the time

5. **I don't expect difficult people to change. I realize that I have to change my response to them if I am to expect a change in their actions toward me.**
   a. Rarely
   b. Sometimes
   c. Most of the time

6. **I am able to control my response when confronted by a difficult person.**
   a. Rarely
   b. Sometimes
   c. Most of the time

7. **I usually listen and acknowledge the difficult person's message.**
   a. Rarely
   b. Sometimes
   c. Most of the time

8. **I focus on problem solving.**
   a. Rarely
   b. Sometimes
   c. Most of the time

9. **I deal directly with the behavior and not with the difficult person's personality.**
   a. Rarely
   b. Sometimes
   c. Most of the time

10. **I often use specific strategies that serve as coping skills with various types of difficult people.**
    a. Rarely
    b. Sometimes
    c. Most of the time

    I would like to learn more about various types of difficult people and how best to handle them.
    A. The "I Know Everything" Type   Yes___   No___
    B. The "Indecisive" Type   Yes___   No___
    C. The "Backstabber" Type   Yes___   No___
    D. The "Bully" Type   Yes___   No___
    E. The "Cronic Complainer" Type   Yes___   No___
    F. The "Explosive" Type   Yes___   No___

Support Staff

Conflict Management
Coaching Tool (form continued)

Name: _____

Dept/School: _____

Date: _____

Scoring Sheet

Most of the Time: 30-26 points
Sometimes: 25-21 points
Rarely: 20 points and below

Most of the Time:

Your conflict management skills are excellent. When confronted with people who continually challenge you, you are able to take action to improve your situation without losing control of your behavior.

Sometimes:

Although you are generally are able to maintain control of a difficult situation, you occassionally lose sight of the real problem and focus on the individual and not on his or her behavior.

Rarely:

You seldom use any strategies that serve as coping skills with various types of difficult people.

Support Staff

Conflict Management
Coaching Tool (form continued)

Name: _____

Dept/School: _____

Date: _____

DEFINE THE PROBLEM:

1. What is the history of the conflict?

2. What is the present cause?

3. Who are the involved parties?

4. What has been tried to resolve the problem?

5. What are the barriers to resolution?

Support Staff

**Conflict Management
Coaching Tool** (form continued)

Name: _____

Dept/School: _____

Date: _____

FOCUS ON SOLUTIONS, NOT ON THE PROBLEM OR THE INDIVIDUAL:

- List three potential options

  1.

  2.

  3.

- Look for win–win situations

  1.

  2.

  3.

- Select the least problematic action

Take Action!!!

- If you perceive a problem, try to resolve it now. Deal directly and discreetly.
- Define the problem.
- Try to bring the parties together by reducing the differences between you. Aim to improve the relationship long term.
- Stay calm and control your response. Don't take it personally.
- Reflect, listen and acknowledge, focus on problem solving, and then give and request frequent feedback. (Be proactive, not reactive.)
- Explain that the situation is a mutual problem to be solved, not a win-lose conflict. Put your efforts into the *relationship* and not on the current difficult situation.
- Try not to take sides. Separate the people from the problem.
- Don't expect difficult people to change.
- Display concern, and let co-workers vent.
- Determine whether or not the situation has major consequences.
- Determine your desired outcome, and define your expectations for after the conflict has been solved. **(Remember: Don't assume that there is only one way to solve a problem!)**
- Document for self-protection. Get potentially troublesome verbal agreements in writing to prevent the other individual from reneging on your solution.

Beware of Common Pitfalls:

- Ignoring the problem, hoping that it will disappear.
- Diving into a conflict too impulsively without reflecting about the consequences.
- Minimizing your coworkers' complaints. (If the situation is a concern for them, it may soon become a crisis for you!)

If all else fails, bring in a mediator.

Support Staff

**Conflict Management
Coaching Tool** (form continued)

Name: _____

Dept/School: _____

Date: _____

COPING STRATEGIES FOR DEALING WITH DIFFICULT PEOPLE

The "I Know Everything" Type:

1. Be knowledgeable about the subject; use "I" statements.
2. Listen attentively and paraphrase what they say.
3. Don't challenge them; ask logical questions to lead them to see their errors.
4. Focus on the solution.
5. Guard against yourself becoming the "expert"; let them be the "experts." They hate to be wrong.

The "Indecisive" Type:

1. Reassure them about relationships; provide a lot of acknowledgment.
2. Make it safe for them to be honest.
3. Help them think through the problem.
4. Surface the potential conflict.
5. Help them prioritize alternatives, but leave action steps in your hands.
6. Work out a win–win solution.
7. Collaboratively set a timeline and get a commitment.
8. Offer them ongoing support.

The "Back Stabber" Type:

1. Gain evidence from others that the behavior is occurring.
2. Expose them, but don't try to get even; let them "save face."
3. Address the behavior directly. Ask them direct questions about what bothers them. They will often retreat if directly questioned about what their sarcasm really means.
4. Confront sarcasm as soon as it occurs.
5. If this happens in a group, ask the group if they agree.
6. Address sniping each time that it occurs until it stops.
7. Try not to overreact.

The "Bully" Type:

1. Stand up for yourself in a noncombative manner.
2. Don't try to augue with him or her.
3. Don't allow yourself to be interrupted.
4. State the facts calmly.
5. Listen to everything he or she has to say, but you may have to interrupt with phrases such as: *"I disagree, but explain your thinking"; "You interrupted me"; "In my opinion . . ."*
6. Be concise and clear with your reactions.
7. Keep control of your emotions. Don't get into a shouting match.
8. Encourage him or her to problem solve with you.

Support Staff

Name: _____

Dept/School: _____

Date: _____

The "Chronic Complainer" Type:

1. Clearly define the issue.

2. Listen and acknowledge, but don't argue. Let him or her reveal all of the negative factors of an idea first and then be specific in your response.

3. Be prepared to interrupt gently; ask questions.

4. State the facts; get him or her to problem solve; don't solve the problem.

5. Ask "Who?," "What?," "When?," and "Where?"—Don't ask "Why?"

6. Suggest some possible alternative solutions.

7. Assign time limits on tasks.

8. Encourage positive interaction. Show him or her "what's in it" for him or her.

The "Explosive" Type:

1. Don't let him or her intimidate you.

2. Talk privately if possible, or leave him or her alone for a while to give time to compose him or herself.

3. When he or she has calmed down, explain that his or her behavior is not acceptable.

4. Ask what can be done to prevent this from happening in the future—and listen carefully!

5. Be formal, concise, clear, and calm with you reactions.

Support Staff

**Conflict Management
Coaching Tool** (form continued)

Name: _____

Dept/School: _____

Date: _____

10 TIPS FOR DEALING WITH HOSTILE AUDIENCES:

1. **Give the irate person 100% of your undivided attention.** Maintain eye contact; keep your facial expressions neutral and your arms open, which tells the upset person that you are open to their opinions.

2. **Be a patient listener. Do not interrupt.** Pause when they have finished. They will be surprised that you didn't get engaged immediately.

3. **Adjust your attitude.** Choose to see the hostile person as a friend who needs more information or additional help.

4. **Ask a clarifying question if you are unclear about their meaning.** This will demonstrate that you want to understand their position.

5. **If the person is very upset, paraphrase back the facts and the feelings that you think you heard.** This lets him or her know that you are listening and trying to understand his or her position.

6. **Apologize if you or your organization hasn't met their expectations**—even if it wasn't your fault.

7. **Show empathy.** Walk in their shoes for a minute. Speak in a sincere and caring tone. Call the person by name.

8. **Communicate the issue as you see it, wearing your "customer advocate" hat.** Focus on what you can do for them. Take a rational, objective approach; then outline the points of agreement.

9. **Ask for his or her ideas for an acceptable next step.** Turn an adversary into a collaborator.

10. **Acknowledge his or her ideas and stay focused on a win–win solution.**

Support Staff

Conflict Management
Coaching Tool (form continued)

Name: _____

Dept/School: _____

Date: _____

Individual Development Plan for
Conflict Management
Select 2–3 goals

Problem to be Improved	Strategies	Date to be Completed
1.		
2.		
3.		

CONFLICT MANAGEMENT REFERENCES

Axelrod, A. (1997) *201 ways to deal with difficult people.* New York: McGraw Hill Trade.

Bramson, R. (1998) *Coping with difficult people.* New York: Dell/Bantam.

Crowe, S. (1999) *Since strangling isn't an option . . . : Dealing with difficult people- Common problems and uncommon solutions.* New York: Perigree.

Faber, A. (1999) *How to talk so kids will listen and listen so kids will talk.* London: Avon Books.

Glass, L. (1995). *Toxic people.* New York: Simon and Schuster.

Mayer, B. (2000) *The dynamics of conflict resolution: A practitioner's guide.* New York: Jossey-Bass.

Soloman, M. (1990). *Working with difficult people.* Englewood Cliffs, NJ: Prentice Hall.

Weeks, D. (1992) *The eight essential steps to conflict management.* New York: P. Jeremy Archer/Putnam.

William, W., & Wilmot, J. (2000) *Interpersonal conflict.* New York: WCB/ McGraw-Hill.

Public Relations Introduction

Support Staff

Name: _____

Dept/School: _____

Date: _____

INTRODUCTION TO PUBLIC RELATIONS

Few school employees today also have been trained to handle the complications of the people part of their jobs. Schools are now challenged to be customer oriented more than ever before. School staffs typically resist the notion of customer, as they believe that that likens them too much to a business environment. In reality, however, that is the current situation for schools. Those schools that provide the best learning environment and experience for children attract the greater number of the students. Thus, the terms *customer* and *customer service* should become permanent words in school staff members' vocabularies.

Moreover, school staffs have not been encouraged to treat people inside their own organizations as well as they treat people outside. They need to become familiar with the terms *internal customer* and *external customer*. **Internal customers receive their work or service from other employees to help them assist the direct customer**. Such customers are all of the individuals with whom you work, both above and below your particular level of employment. **External customers are the people that receive your direct service**. All school employees' direct customers are the students and their parents, as well as the community at large. However, just to help finesse your eventually grasping this concept of customer service, let's use the terms *internal public relations skills* and *external public relations skills* instead of customer service skills.

Unfortunately, frontline employees in K-12 education see themselves as in the left triangle, when in reality, they represent the first contact for external customers.

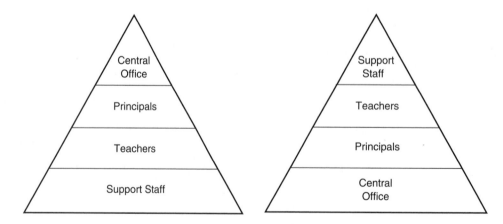

Support Staff

Public Relations Introduction
(form continued)

Name: _____

Dept/School: _____

Date: _____

The frontline worker is the most important person and the first contact the external customer has with the school. One never gets a second chance to make a first impression, so it is essential that he or she meets the individual's needs positively and efficiently. As parents send schools the best children that they have, school employees must exert the best effort they can to meet the needs of those students. One must have a thorough knowledge of the organization; a positive working relationship with co-workers; excellent time and stress management skills; a willingness to take ownership of a problem; and a commitment to students, school, and work in general. Support staff should dress so others will feel comfortable; not surround themselves with clutter; be respectful of their team members; not eat or drink in their work areas if they are in a highly visible locations; and most important, be positive about the organization.

All staff must also be excellent listeners. Everyone should listen using empathy, acknowledge what they understand the sender's message to be, and be able to paraphrase back to the individual what they understood him or her to say. They should speak slowly in a calm tone and always identify themselves. They should also listen to the content of the sender's message and keep it separate from the emotion of the situation. In tense situations, they should remember that an individual's hostility is merely a symptom, not the problem. Everyone should try to not take words and actions personally!

For example, there are 10 basic steps that one should follow when dealing with a difficult individual:

1. Acknowledge the person's concerns and feelings. Show that you have a genuine interest in his or her well-being.

2. Create an atmosphere of openness, honesty, and integrity.

3. Develop a sense of mutual respect between employees and customers.

4. Use active listening techniques.

5. Apologize, if appropriate.

6. Show that you value the individual.

7. Ask questions for information to better understand the issue. If you cannot solve his or her problem, then find someone else within the organization who can.

8. Explore options that are acceptable to both you and the individual.

9. Thank the person for bringing the problem to your attention. Through this initiative, he or she has given you another chance to solve the problem.

10. Be flexible! Show people that you will do everything possible to meet their needs.

Support Staff

Public Relations Coaching Tool

Name: _____

Dept/School: _____

Date: _____

Self-Appraisal: Public Relations Skills

1. **I understand the meaning of the terms *internal* and *external* public relations.**
   a. Rarely
   b. Sometimes
   c. Most of the time

2. **I listen with empathy and for solutions to all peoples' problems.**
   a. Rarely
   b. Sometimes
   c. Most of the time

3. **I encourage feedback.**
   a. Rarely
   b. Sometimes
   c. Most of the time

4. **I pay attention to details.**
   a. Rarely
   b. Sometimes
   c. Most of the time

5. **I develop and encourage repeat relationships.**
   a. Rarely
   b. Sometimes
   c. Most of the time

6. **I value the individual's time and do not squander it unnecessarily.**
   a. Rarely
   b. Sometimes
   c. Most of the time

7. **I seek to exceed people's expectations.**
   a. Rarely
   b. Sometimes
   c. Most of the time

8. **It is possible for me to be pleasant to people who are indifferent to me.**
   a. Rarely
   b. Sometimes
   c. Most of the time

9. **I do not mind apologizing for mistakes even though I did not make them.**
   a. Rarely
   b. Sometimes
   c. Most of the time

10. **I am strong in remembering names and faces, and I make efforts to improve this skill when meeting others.**
    a. Rarely
    b. Sometimes
    c. Most of the time

Support Staff

Public Relations
Coaching Tool (form continued)

Name: _____

Dept/School: _____

Date: _____

11. **I consistently try to go above and beyond what is expected.**
    a. Rarely
    b. Sometimes
    c. Most of the time

12. **I try to be flexible and empathetic when working with difficult people.**
    a. Rarely
    b. Sometimes
    c. Most of the time

13. **I share information with my colleagues about what our students', staffs', and parents' needs and wants are.**
    a. Rarely
    b. Sometimes
    c. Most of the time

14. **I follow-up on problems to ensure that they have been resolved.**
    a. Rarely
    b. Sometimes
    c. Most of the time

15. **If I cannot solve a person's problem, I put the individual in touch with someone who can.**
    a. Rarely
    b. Sometimes
    c. Most of the time

16. **I feel ownership and responsibility for the quality of service I provide people.**
    a. Rarely
    b. Sometimes
    c. Most of the time

17. **In meeting others' needs, employees in my work group work well together.**
    a. Rarely
    b. Sometimes
    c. Most of the time

18. **I have a sense of satisfaction when I meet a person's needs.**
    a. Rarely
    b. Sometimes
    c. Most of the time

19. **I believe that complaints are actually a second chance to correct a problem.**
    a. Rarely
    b. Sometimes
    c. Most of the time

20. **I realize that I have an important public relations role in this organization.**
    a. Rarely
    b. Sometimes
    c. Most of the time

Support Staff

Public Relations Coaching Tool (form continued)

Name: _____

Dept/School: _____

Date: _____

Scoring Sheet for Public Relations Skills

A = 1 point
B = 2 points
C = 3 points

Most of the Time: 30-26 points
Sometimes: 25-21 points
Rarely: 20 points and below

Most of the Time:

I have a good understanding of the role of public relations in the organization and how all of the members of the school interact on behalf of student learning. I listen carefully to people's concerns and try to help them get solutions to their problems. If I cannot help the individual, I never fail to try to get someone else in the organization to do so. I get great satisfaction from meeting and exceeding people's expectations.

Sometimes:

I usually respond empathetically to people's concerns, but I sometimes fail to pay attention to details or to paraphrase back to the individual what I thought he or she said. I also sometimes have difficulty dealing with difficult people.

Rarely:

I don't understand my public relations role in the school setting. I sometimes resent having to try to meet people's demands constantly, and if I can't solve a person's problems, I tell him or her so. I value my time more than other people's time.

Support Staff

**Public Relations
Coaching Tool** (form continued)

Name: _____

Dept/School: _____

Date: _____

PRACTICES THAT MAKE A DIFFERENCE IN PUBLIC RELATIONS

- Realize that you have only one chance to make a first impression!
- Introduce yourself immediately and ask how you can be of help.
- Be effective public relations role models. Remember, you represent the entire organization!
- Be committed to providing outstanding service.
- Refer people to others in the school when you don't have answers to specific questions.
- Identify any barriers to your ability to provide exceptional service, and work with your supervisors and colleagues to remove those barriers.
- Help coworkers to feel ownership, responsibility, and pride for and in their work.
- Do more than the minimum required, and try to exceed expectations.
- Measure the success of efforts to improve service quality.
- Do not make other people feel invisible.
- Make it a practice to look people in the eye during face-to-face interactions.
- Be empathetic and treat others as you would want to be treated.
- Make an honest effort to help others.
- Talk less and listen more.
- Make it a priority to understand other people's needs.
- Pay attention to people's body language and their other nonverbal cues.
- Ask for feedback regarding the quality of your service.
- Pay attention to details that matter to other people.
- Try to develop ongoing, repeat relationships.
- Respond effectively and efficiently to people's problems.
- Pay attention to small details that matter to people.
- Have confidence in service received by other parts of the organization.
- Encourage colleagues to set personal service examples.
- Ask customers what they expect.
- Take responsibility for day-to-day techniques needed to deliver service.
- Refer people to others in the organization if you cannot help them.
- Maintain a positive attitude!

Support Staff

Public Relations
Coaching Tool (form continued)

Name: _____

Dept/School: _____

Date: _____

PRACTICES THAT MAKE A DIFFERENCE IN CREATING COLLEGIAL ENVIRONMENTS FOR STUDENTS

- Establish and maintain good rapport with all students. Let students know that you care about them.
- Communicate tactfully, courteously, patiently, and effectively with students.
- Serve as advocates for students.
- Learn students' names as quickly as you can.
- Encourage students to share their problems. Try to generally maintain confidentiality. However, find help for them if necessary.
- Be observant; listen carefully.
- Make a conscious effort to reach out to students who are troubled or very shy. Compliment or acknowledge them whenever you see them.
- Be reliable. This basis for trust is the foundation for lasting relationships. "Walk the talk," and be consistent and fair with all students.
- Be a role model regarding lifestyle, values, attitudes, hobbies, and interests for students.
- Participate in a Big Brothers/Big Sisters Program.
- Remember that students, like adults, are interested in themselves, and they want to be acknowledged, to feel important, and to be appreciated.
- Know the school, staff, and program well. If you are not able to provide answers to students' questions, be able to refer the students to someone who can help them.
- Try to directly impact student learning. For example, paraprofessionals can supervise and train students to run a peer mediation program; food service workers can teach a unit on nutrition to students; bus drivers can be student mentors; all support staff can read frequently to students.
- Exhibit good judgment and initiative in emergency situations.
- Be available to help in personal emergencies, such as students being locked out of their cars or helping a student with a problem on the playground.
- Pay constant attention to all safety conditions in the school.
- Help students respect themselves and their school facilities.
- Assist with the supervision of authorized student activities when requested.
- Provide a direct link between jobs that are done in the school every day and the students' ability to thrive and learn.
- Participate in school improvement and crisis intervention teams, and demonstrate your unique perspectives to students, staff, and parents alike.
- Attend school board meetings to raise the awareness of important specific school issues and concerns from your perspective.
- On "Career Day" volunteer to talk to classes about your specific job and how it helps enable them to learn in a safe, orderly, attractive, friendly environment.
- Establish positive relationships with parents!

Support Staff

Public Relations
Coaching Tool (form continued)

Name: _____

Dept/School: _____

Date: _____

Individual Development Plan
for Public Relations
Select 2–3 goals

Problem to be Improved	Strategies	Date to be Completed
1.		
2.		
3.		

PUBLIC RELATIONS REFERENCES

Bhote, K. (1996). *Beyond customer satisfaction to customer loyalty.* New York: American Management Association.

Cannie, J. (1991). *Keeping customers for life.* New York: AMACOM.

Chang, R., & Kelly, P. (1994). *Satisfying internal customers first.* Los Angeles: Richard Chang Associates.

Cowan, J. (2002) *Techniques for communicators.* Chicago: Lawrence Ragan Communications.

Finch, L. (1994). *Twenty ways to improve customer service.* Menlo Park, CA: CRISP Publications.

Gerson, R. (1992). *Beyond customer service.* Menlo Park, CA: CRISP Publications.

Harvey, E. (1999). *180 ways to walk the customer service talk.* Dallas, TX: Performance Publishing.

Morgan, R. (1989). *Calming upset customers.* Menlo Park, CA: CRISP Publications.

Temme, J. (1994). *Total quality customer service: How to make it your way of life.* Mission, KS: Skillpath Publications.

Zemke, R., & Anderson, K. (1998). *Delivering knock your socks off service.* King of Prussia, PA: Performance Research Associates.

Support Staff

Stress Management Introduction

Name: _____

Dept/School: _____

Date: _____

INTRODUCTION TO STRESS MANAGEMENT

All of us are aware of stress and of the very negative images of time-crunched people trying to cram more tasks into less time, working in difficult situations and with challenging people, not liking our jobs, and so on. We can also recognize that we all face western society's constant expectations to be successful and productive, while risking our enjoyment of our lives as well as our own physical, mental, and spiritual health!

This response to stress is not a new phenomenon. From the caveman's existence to the present day we have learned that human beings have a *fight or flight* response. This was the caveman's first reaction and capacity to respond to danger. Just as in the past a "stressor" is any external event (a new job, a marriage, a divorce, moving to a new city, etc.) that makes you uncertain and feeling out of control. Today we are now coping with perceived threats that are more likely mental than physical, and that make us feel stressed. Stress itself is not harmful. *It is how you react to stress that can be harmful to your life!* You need to be able to respond appropriately to a variety of different stressors. If you don't do this, you may fall victim to heart and intestinal disease, increased risk for cancer, stroke, diabetes, and a host of minor illnesses such as colds, headaches, backaches, and insomnia.

Response to stress has frequently been discussed in terms of Type A and Type B personalities. A person with a Type A personality usually has intense drive and ambition, is competitive, needs to get projects or tasks done and to meet deadlines, is visibly restless, impatient, and sometimes can be hostile. A person with a Type B personality, on the other hand, has an easy going manner, is usually patient, takes the time to enjoy life, is not ruled by the clock, and is much less competitive than the Type A personality. Research has demonstrated in several studies that individuals with Type A personalities develop coronary artery disease 2.5 times as often as people with Type B personalities!

The reaction to stressors can also be determined by sex. A man may feel stressed if he has not attained his career goals by a mid-point in his life. A high-achieving woman, on the other hand, often is stressed by her success, as she feels guilty about possibly having neglected her family to progress in her career.

However, both men and women respond in a stressful manner if they have jobs in which high demands are placed on them, and they have little control over how best to accomplish their responsibilities. These jobs often are in the service areas, where a high demand on concentrated repetition exists without the opportunity for independent thinking, or where they have to try to satisfy customers without ever having the chance to give their frontline input on how to improve procedures. Moreover, employees in these sectors often have little to no social and emotional support while they are on the job.

Support Staff

Name: _____

Dept/School: _____

Date: _____

Finally, many employees are stressed by their constant efforts to keep up with technology, as well as to remain competitive in the workplace. They are afraid of losing their jobs and of becoming one more statistic on the evening news.

Organizations need to give their employees more control over their jobs and their work environments. Concrete examples of this are offering flexible working hours, enabling personalized work areas, and participation in school improvement teams.

Employees need to try to complement their school's efforts with their own personalized stress management techniques. They need to develop a support group; to practice effective time management skills; to learn how to be assertive without being aggressive or rude; to use effective communication techniques; and to encourage supportive and personalized work areas. They also should exercise regularly; practice relaxation techniques; pay attention to their overall health and nutrition; develop hobbies; and involve themselves in their family activities. Through all of these approaches, people can regain their sense of humor, start to enjoy their free time again, and most important, begin to feel that they are in control.

Support Staff

Stress Management
Coaching Tool

Name: _____

Dept/School: _____

Date: _____

Stress Management Self-Analysis

Write down three major stresses in your work. How do you typically respond to these stressors?

1.

2.

3.

Write down three to five common daily occurrences that aggravate you. How do you typically respond to these stressors?

1.

2.

3.

4.

5.

Remember, stress itself is not the problem; it is your reaction to an event or to an individual that causes the physical or psychological problems!

Support Staff

Stress Management
Coaching Tool (form continued)

Name: _____

Dept/School: _____

Date: _____

Symptoms of Stress in the Workplace:

YES	NO	
❏	❏	I am tired all of the time.
❏	❏	I have trouble sleeping at night.
❏	❏	I experience frequent headaches, backaches, or chest pain.
❏	❏	I cry frequently.
❏	❏	I can't effectively handle several problems or tasks at once.
❏	❏	I have difficulty controlling my temper when criticized or provoked.
❏	❏	I frequently feel out of control or overwhelmed.
❏	❏	I am often irritable, cynical, and negative.
❏	❏	I am a perfectionist.
❏	❏	I am often depressed.
❏	❏	I depend on alcohol, drugs, or both.
❏	❏	I often have conflicts with my family members.
❏	❏	I have no leisure activities.
❏	❏	I am frequently ill at ease in social situations.
❏	❏	I constantly worry about something.
❏	❏	I am experiencing burnout on the job.

How Do I Know I Am Burned Out?

YES	NO	
❏	❏	I consistently work long hours.
❏	❏	People tell me I look tired all of the time.
❏	❏	I dread going to work.
❏	❏	I have lost my appetite or eat everything in sight.
❏	❏	I am frequently ill.
❏	❏	I am often bored.
❏	❏	I am impatient or irritable.
❏	❏	I am not able to concentrate.
❏	❏	I am negative in all or most situations.
❏	❏	I am not confident.
❏	❏	I tend to blame others for problems.

Support Staff

Name: _____

Dept/School: _____

Date: _____

HOW TO DEAL WITH BURNOUT:

- Ask your supervisor to provide training and support.
- Express your negative feelings.
- Admit your mistakes.
- Try to eliminate the conflict between your supervisor's demands and your needs and abilities.
- Be orderly in your work habits.
- Use effective time management strategies.
- Set realistic goals with reasonable deadlines for yourself! **Remember: it is important to take time to heal and recover from burnout.**
- Get career counseling.
- Develop a continuing education plan for yourself (i.e., time management or anger management class).
- Try to regain your sense of humor. Remember, "Before you embark on a journey of revenge, dig two graves." —Booker T. Washington

Support Staff

Stress Management
Coaching Tool (form continued)

Name: _____

Dept/School: _____

Date: _____

Four Ways to Cope With Stress

1. Change your internal attitude and perceptions.

- Turn anxiety into opportunity:
  - Take control by getting organized
  - Assess what is important and then do it
  - Learn to not waste time on little things that don't matter
  - Take care of yourself emotionally and physically
  - Choose work that is personally meaningful to you whenever possible
  - Be open to change
- Set aside quiet time for yourself to meditate, write, think, etc.
- Develop social supports that reduce your sense of aloneness.
- Develop a sense of humor about your situation.
- Talk about your difficulties with your friends.
- Seek professional counseling.
- Take responsibility for your own stress.
- Know yourself and your level of optimum stress.

2. Change your interaction with the environment.

- Improve your skills in areas like goal setting, time management, and conflict management.
- Take assertiveness training.
- Use peer feedback as a way to identify areas for possible changes in your behavior.
- Slow down and think before you act!

3. Change your physical ability to cope.

- Find a balance between time for yourself and time for others.
- Believe in a set of values external to yourself.
- Get adequate and proper nutrition.
- Start a fitness program.
- Reduce your intake of caffeine, nicotine, alcohol, and sugar.
- Get enough sleep and rest.
- Develop some recreational activities.

4. Change your environment.

- Stop attending meetings or being with people who upset you.
- Change your job/vocation/location
- Take classes to learn new skills and develop new interests.
- Structure time off from work.
- Set up your job, if possible, so you can work in a variety of different program areas.

Support Staff

Name: _____

Dept/School: _____

Date: _____

Strategies to Improve Your Coping Skills

1. **To improve your problem-solving skills (*your ability to face directly difficult situations and take positive action to resolve them*):**

   - If you perceive a problem, then try to define it accurately.
   - Gather and evaluate relevant data.
   - Separate people from the problem.
   - Separate emotions from the problem.
   - Establish your desired outcome.
   - Provide a variety of creative and practical solutions.
   - Choose the best alternatives given the realities of the situation.
   - Develop a plan for implementing your solution.

2. **To improve your communication skills (*your ability to share your thoughts and feelings with others to enable mutual understanding in comfortable and challenging situations*):**

   - Listen to understand, not to judge.
   - Focus on the message sent, not on the messenger.
   - Use reflective listening, so that you are able to provide accurate feedback to the speaker.
   - Use "I" statements when you speak.
   - Be assertive, not aggressive.
   - Speak with a purpose.
   - Ask for feedback.
   - Believe in yourself.

3. **To improve your relationships with friends, family, and colleagues (*your ability to develop a supportive social network in each area of your life—personal, family, and work*):**

   - Make relationships a priority.
   - Share your personal feelings.
   - Develop a support system; make quality time for key people in your life.
   - Focus on the positive and give praise when it's deserved.

4. **To improve your ability to be flexible and deal effectively with change (*your ability to be comfortable in structured, predictable situations and in unstructured, unpredictable situations*):**

   - Be open to different ideas; see the merits of perspectives other than your own.
   - Brainstorm ideas without judging them.
   - Put yourself in other people's roles to better understand their behavior.
   - Learn to adapt to change, and learn to accept the things you cannot change.
   - Switch to a different strategy when an old one is unsuccessful.
   - Be willing to modify a strongly held position in the face of valid, reliable evidence
   - Don't let minor irritations cause you stress.
   - Focus on your future.

Support Staff

Stress Management
Coaching Tool (form continued)

Name: _____

Dept/School: _____

Date: _____

Individual Development
Plan for Stress Management
Select 2–3 goals

Problem to be Improved	Strategies	Date to be Completed
1.		
2.		
3.		

STRESS MANAGEMENT REFERENCES

Bensen, H., & Stuart, E. (1992) *The wellness book: A comprehensive guide to maintaining health treating stress-related illness.* New York: Simon and Schuster.

Carson, G. (1988). *Winning ways: Techniques that take you to the top.* New York: The Berkeley Publishing Group.

Charlesworth, E., & Nathan, R. (1991). *Stress management: A comprehensive guide to wellness.* New York: Ballantine Books.

Eliot, R. (1994). *From stress to strength.* New York: Berkley Publishing Group.

Friedman, M., & Rosenman, R. (1974). *Type A behavior and your heart.* Greenwich, CT: Fawcett.

Goliszek, A. (1987). *Breaking the stress habit.* Winston Salem, NC: Caroline Press.

Hanson, P. (1989). *Stress for success.* New York: Doubleday.

Kriegel, R., & Kriegel, M. (1984). *The C zone: Peak performance under pressure.* Garden City, New York: Anchor Press/Doubleday.

Merrill, F. (1984). *The female stress syndrome: How to recognize and live with it.* New York: New Market Press.

Pritchett, P., & Pound, R. *The stress of organizational change.* Dallas, TX: Pritchett and Associates.

Sehnert, K. (1991). *Stress/unstress: How you can control stress at home and on the job.* Minneapolis, MN: Augsburg Press.

Witkin-Lanoil, G. (1986). *The male stress syndrome.* New York: New Market Press.

Team Building Introduction

Support Staff

Name: _____

Dept/School: _____

Date: _____

INTRODUCTION TO TEAM BUILDING

In order to understand the importance of working in a team environment, one must first understand the meaning of the word "team." *A team is a number of people who are committed to a common purpose, performance goals, and approach for which they hold themselves mutually accountable.* Because each member makes a unique contribution, a team offers a great deal of potential. Essentially, with an effective team, the whole is greater than the sum of its parts.

Therefore, it is critical that you create your teams on the basis of complementary skills whenever possible. Although all problems or projects cannot be best handled by a team, those circumstances that would benefit from a team model are:

- When a variety of skills and talents would be beneficial in solving the problem
- When a sense of togetherness is lacking in the work environment
- When poor communication is inherent in the organization
- When an atmosphere of competition, not cooperation, exists
- When a solution that is unpopular to some but is the wish of the majority needs to be implemented

There are five key elements of a team that are represented by the five "C's":

1. Commitment
2. Competence
3. Challenging work
4. Control over work
5. Cooperation

In order to gain commitment from every team member, you need to clarify, discuss, and evaluate every team member's expectations on a regular basis in order to avoid disappointment. You must also share your expectations for a team's performance based on the following major areas:

- Information is open and honest; flows freely up, down, and sideways
- People relationships are trusting, respectful, collaborative, and supportive
- Conflict is regarded as a natural, even helpful method of getting feedback if it's focused on issues and not on people
- Atmosphere is open, nonthreatening, noncompetitive, and participative
- Decisions are made by consensus and require full commitment
- Creativity generates many options that are solution oriented
- Power base is shared by all team members based on their competence in specific skill areas and on their contribution to the team
- Motivation is increased by having team members' belonging needs satisfied
- Rewards are based on contribution to group and on peer recognition

Support Staff

Team Building Introduction
(form continued)

Name: _____

Dept/School: _____

Date: _____

On an effective team there is a common understanding of the individual skills and abilities that each team member brings to the unit, the importance of the work, shared leadership roles, the common goals and the commitment from all team members to these goals, open-ended discussion and active problem-solving sessions, collaborative work products, specific measurements for assessing their collective work products, and mutual accountability. Management at all levels must support team efforts openly and without reservation if it expects it to succeed.

In order for any team to meet its goals:

- Make sure that goals are clearly communicated and understood.
- Provide opportunities to meet and exchange ideas with team members.
- Treat employees with equal respect and give each an opportunity to make a personal contribution to the outcome.
- Act consistently and positively.
- Stay calm under pressure.
- Keep all promises made to team members.

Finally, there are 10 major components of productive teams:

1. Team goals are as important as individual goals
2. Team members understand the goals and are committed to achieving them; everyone is willing to share responsibilities
3. Team climate is comfortable and informal; people feel empowered; individual competitiveness is inappropriate.
4. Communication is spontaneous and shared; diversity of opinions and ideas is encouraged.
5. Respect, open-mindedness, collaboration are highly valued; members seek a win–win solution and they build on each other's ideas.
6. Trust replaces fear; team members feel comfortable taking risks.
7. Conflicts and differences of opinions are considered opportunities to explore new ideas; the emphasis is always on finding common ground.
8. Team procedures, processes, and practices are continually reviewed.
9. Leadership is rotated; no one person dominates the team.
10. Decisions are made by consensus and have the acceptance and support of all team members.

Creating and supporting a team can be a challenging experience, though the benefits clearly outweigh the risks and hard work. By working closely with one another in a collegial manner, you will have created a special interrelatedness among team members that would have otherwise not existed. Your teammates are your assets and your friends as you go about the organization's work. Maximize every individual's potential on behalf of your entire school.

Support Staff

**Team Building
Coaching Tool**

Name: _____

Dept/School: _____

Date: _____

Self-Appraisal

1. **I work well with a wide range of people.**
   a. Rarely _____
   b. Sometimes _____
   c. Most of the time _____

2. **I find ways for others to contribute to the goals of my team.**
   a. Rarely _____
   b. Sometimes _____
   c. Most of the time _____

3. **I try to support the members of my team in a way that is never negative toward other team members.**
   a. Rarely _____
   b. Sometimes _____
   c. Most of the time _____

4. **I take a leadership role whenever possible.**
   a. Rarely _____
   b. Sometimes _____
   c. Most of the time _____

5. **I can make other coworkers' ideas work in real situations.**
   a. Rarely _____
   b. Sometimes _____
   c. Most of the time _____

6. **I am able to appraise others' ideas objectively.**
   a. Rarely _____
   b. Sometimes _____
   c. Most of the time _____

7. **I am not afraid to be outspoken when I feel I am right.**
   a. Rarely _____
   b. Sometimes _____
   c. Most of the time _____

8. **I like meetings to be organized and well run.**
   a. Rarely _____
   b. Sometimes _____
   c. Most of the time _____

9. **I enjoy when my team brainstorms solutions to problems.**
   a. Rarely _____
   b. Sometimes _____
   c. Most of the time _____

10. **I am likely to show my impatience with people who block progress.**
    a. Rarely _____
    b. Sometimes _____
    c. Most of the time _____

11. **My tendency to be a perfectionist sometimes creates delays for my team.**
    a. Rarely _____
    b. Sometimes _____
    c. Most of the time _____

12. **I often try to contribute something original to my team.**
    a. Rarely _____
    b. Sometimes _____
    c. Most of the time _____

Support Staff

Team Building
Coaching Tool (form continued)

Name: _____

Dept/School: _____

Date: _____

13. **I try to support all valuable suggestions made in a team discussion.**
    a. Rarely _____
    b. Sometimes _____
    c. Most of the time _____

14. **I try to keep my team on schedule.**
    a. Rarely _____
    b. Sometimes _____
    c. Most of the time _____

15. **I am interested in everyone's point of view.**
    a. Rarely _____
    b. Sometimes _____
    c. Most of the time _____

16. **I can be relied upon to complete my responsibilities in a team effort**
    a. Rarely _____
    b. Sometimes _____
    c. Most of the time _____

17. **I can usually get my team members to agree on action.**
    a. Rarely _____
    b. Sometimes _____
    c. Most of the time _____

18. **I can find practical solutions to problems.**
    a. Rarely _____
    b. Sometimes _____
    c. Most of the time _____

19. **I sometimes inhibit others' contributions by making critical judgments too often.**
    a. Rarely _____
    b. Sometimes _____
    c. Most of the time _____

20. **I can find compromises to resolve conflicts between people.**
    a. Rarely _____
    b. Sometimes _____
    c. Most of the time _____

21. **I like to encourage good working relationships on my team.**
    a. Rarely _____
    b. Sometimes _____
    c. Most of the time _____

22. **When I work on a difficult task, I find out what each member of my team can best contribute.**
    a. Rarely _____
    b. Sometimes _____
    c. Most of the time _____

23. **I am rather adaptable and I deal with change well.**
    a. Rarely _____
    b. Sometimes _____
    c. Most of the time _____

24. **I continually try to learn new skills that will enhance my participation on my team.**
    a. Rarely _____
    b. Sometimes _____
    c. Most of the time _____

Support Staff

**Team Building
Coaching Tool** (form continued)

Name: _____

Dept/School: _____

Date: _____

Scoring Sheet

Team Building Skills:

Most of the Time: **60-52 points**
Sometimes: **51-43 points**
Rarely: **43 points and below**

A = 3 points
B = 2 points
C = 1 point

Most of the Time:

You consistently work well with a variety of people, and you try to support your team members whenever possible. You are a natural leader, and you often try to incorporate your teammates' ideas into a project. Finally, you motivate people well, and you model desired behavior for all members of your team.

Sometimes:

You like to work with different people, but at times you lose patience with them if you see them as incompetent, stubborn, or lacking in time and organizational management skills.

Rarely:

You don't like to work with people who have a work style that is different from yours. You tend to show your impatience with other members' creativity, and you let them know how you feel through your verbal and nonverbal behavior. You may not like conflict, but you often engage in negative interpersonal behavior.

Support Staff

**Team Building
Coaching Tool** (form continued)

Name: _____

Dept/School: _____

Date: _____

- **Another Definition of "Team":**
  A number of people with complementary skills who are committed to a common purpose, performance goals, and approach for which they hold themselves mutually accountable.

- ***Team member expectations should be surfaced, discussed, and evaluated on a regular basis to avoid disappointment.***

Effective Team Features

- **Objectives:**
These are shared and supported by all team members.
- **Communication:**
This is absolutely necessary and includes feelings as well as contents, such as task-related information. Team members need to understand each other's work styles, preferences, and skills so that they can build on one another's strengths.
- **Leadership:**
This is not held onto by a formal leader, but is widely distributed and shared among all team members. A participated style is adopted.
- **Conflict:**
This is seen as a natural consequence of involvement. Teams should at their very beginning establish ground rules and goals. Conflict is openly expressed and resolved, and it is seen as a positive source of higher quality solutions.
- **Decision Making:**
Decisions are reached on the basis of open debate through processes in which ideas are amended according to the nature of the decision and the impact on or the importance to the group. True teams require time, freedom, and resources to direct their own activities. Decisions must be measurable in order for the team to be held accountable.
- **Interpersonal Relationships:**
These are emphasized to enhance team cohesiveness. Each individual team member is valued equally for his or her unique contribution to the group.
- **Monitoring and Review:**
The ongoing evaluation of the team's effectiveness to ensure continual teamwork improvement.
- **Common Beliefs:**
Team members believe in themselves, in their work, in each other, and in many possibilities.

Effective Team Characteristics

- **Information:**
Is open and honest, and flows freely—up, down, and sideways.
- **Interpersonal Relationships:**
Are trusting, respectful, collaborative, and supportive.
- **Conflict:**
Is accepted as natural and focuses on issues and not individuals.
- **Atmosphere:**
Is open, nonthreatening, noncompetitive, and participative.
- **Decisions:**
Are made by consensus, efficiently utilizing resources and involving every team member in the discussion.
- **Creativity:**
Should be encouraged and solution oriented.
- **Power Base:**
Shared by all and based on competence and one's contribution to the team.
- **Motivation:**
Goals set and supported by team members, belonging needs are satisfied, and accountability is shared.
- **Continual Development of New Work:**
Combined efforts of all team members produces new work generated by team members' decision-making efforts.
- **Rewards:**
Based on contribution to the team and on peer recognition.

Support Staff

Name: _____

Dept/School: _____

Date: _____

TEAM BUILDING EXPECTATIONS

Team Building Behavioral Characteristics:

- **Effort and Consistency:** Individual works for the common good of the team in an organized, diligent, and reliable manner.
- **Attitude:** Individual responds to questions with professional courtesy, is open and honest, shares information with all team members, and builds trust within the team.
- **Contribution and Commitment:** Individual provides positive support that contributes to the goals of the team in a direct or indirect manner.
- **Ownership:** Individual works in a collegial way to achieve outcomes that require teamwork. Individual takes ownership for his or her job within the established team goals.
- **Shows Respect:** Individual supports the members of the team in a way that is never negative toward other team members.
- **Communication:** Individual effectively solicits input from team members and provides feedback to and from team members through writing or in person-to-person communications.
- **Interpersonal:** Individual cooperates and works well with superiors, subordinates, coworkers, and external contacts, and shares leadership when appropriate.
- **Professional Growth:** Individual thrives to learn new team skills.
- **Conflict:** Individual manages conflict to enhance team performance and turns conflict into opportunities to generate new ideas and strengthen relationships.
- **Adaptability:** Individual accepts and contributes to new situations and changes.

Support Staff

Team Building
Coaching Tool (form continued)

Name: _____

Dept/School: _____

Date: _____

Individual Development
Plan for Team Building
Select 2–3 goals

Problem to be Improved	Strategies	Date to be Completed
1.		
2.		
3.		

TEAM BUILDING REFERENCES

Biech, E. (ed.). (2001). *The Pfeiffer book of successful team-building tools: Best of the annuals.* New York: Jossey-Bass/Pfeiffer.

Harper, A., & Harper, B. (1994). *Team barriers: Actions for overcoming the blocks to empowerment, involvement, and high performance.* New York: MW Corporation.

Harrington-Mackin, D. (1994). *The team building toolkit: Tips, tactics, and rules for effective workplace teams.* New York: AMACOM.

Isgar, T. (1989). *The ten minute team: 10 steps to building high performing teams.* Boulder, CO: Seluera Press.

Katzenbach, J., & Smith, D. (1993). *The wisdom of teams: Creating the high-performance organization.* Boston, MA: Harvard Business School Press.

Maddux, R. (1992). *Team building: An exercise in leadership.* Menlo Park, CA: CRISP Publications.

Mallory, C. (1991). *Team building: How to build a winning team.* Shawnee Mission, KS: National Press Publications.

Payne, V. (2001). *The team building workshop.* New York: AMACOM.

Quick, T. (1992). *Successful team building.* New York: AMACOM.

Senge, P., Kleiner, A., Roberts, C., Ross, R., & Smith, B. (1994). *The fifth discipline fieldbook: Strategies and tools for building a learning organization.* New York: Doubleday.

Torres, C., Fairbanks, C., & Roe, R. (ed.). (1996). *Teambuilding.* New York: McGraw Hill.

Support Staff

Time Management Introduction

Name: _____

Dept/School: _____

Date: _____

INTRODUCTION TO TIME MANAGEMENT

When we talk about time management, we think we can actually control time as well as how we use it. However, in reality time is finite; there will always be just 24 hours in a day, 60 minutes in an hour, and 60 seconds in a minute. *What we really are thinking about is how we manage ourselves to best use the time we have.*

How often do we "catch ourselves" wasting time? What are some typical time wasters?

- Handling paper work inefficiently
- Getting bogged down with e-mail
- Making extended/unnecessary telephone calls
- Enabling drop-in visitors
- Addressing unexpected problems or work
- Overscheduling ourselves
- Making mistakes in haste ("Haste makes waste")
- Putting other people's priorities first or allowing their problems to become our emergencies
- Having inability to say "No"
- Allowing unscheduled meetings to take control of your time
- Being too tired to work effectively or efficiently

If you can first *recognize* these time wasters, then you should then begin to plan to minimize or eliminate them. This entire planning process begins with setting specific, doable, realistic goals that can be measured. Also, be aware of your need to prioritize your goals. When reflecting on your work, consider your energy level and at what time of day you work best at difficult tasks. There is no one best time. You know yourself better than anyone else does, so use your best work time to do the project or task that is most difficult for you to do and your least productive work time to do the more or less mundane responsibilities of reading mail, answering e-mail, returning phone calls, and straightening your work space. The key is to match your energy level to the specific task for maximum efficiency.

When creating your work plan, remember to:

- Write down the main components of your plan
- Schedule your time in generous "blocks" of time to allow for some delays
- Review your plan regularly and revise it as necessary
- Divide larger projects into smaller tasks in order to more easily enable their completion
- Complete the more difficult work first
- Create a backup plan to implement only in an emergency

Support Staff

Time Management Introduction
(form continued)

Name: _____

Dept/School: _____

Date: _____

There are many techniques to help us better utilize our time: the daily to-do list; long- and short-term planning; prioritizing our goals and then making sure that everything we do contributes to our success in attaining those goals; tips for avoiding procrastination; hints for conducting effective meetings; ways to delegate; hints for how to say "No"; ways to handle paperwork; and others.

However, handling tasks and handling people require different, more interpersonal skills. For example, how do you handle drop-in visitors without offending them?

- Remain standing when people drop in your area.
- Tell the person you are busy and that you can give him or her only 2 minutes at this time.
- If possible, rearrange your workspace so that your chair does not face the door.
- Ask him or her if you can talk and walk and take care of an errand.
- Refer him or her to a better resource than yourself.
- Don't have chairs available in your work area.

What are some tips for handling telephone interruptions?

- Forward your calls to voicemail when you need undisturbed time.
- Let people know the best time of day to call you.
- Train people to be specific about what information they need from you.
- Leave detailed messages when you return calls.
- Make all of your return phone calls in the same block of time.
- Have your calendar nearby to schedule or to change appointments.
- Stand when you make phone calls.
- Keep "small talk" to a minimum.
- If you or the other party is not fully prepared for a phone conference, reschedule.
- If you are not available, leave a voicemail message regarding when you will return and an alternate contact, if possible.

In selecting the techniques you need to master, you must first reflect on which areas you need the most work. Be honest with yourself, as the time management process is very personal and must fit your work style and situation. When you try to change old habits, it will require a continual awareness on your part to stop doing what you used to do in the way you used to do it. Remember—you are in control of your time. Spend it wisely!

Support Staff

**Time Management
Coaching Tool**

Name: _____

Dept/School: _____

Date: _____

Self-Analysis Tool—Time Management

Task	Often	Sometimes	Rarely
1. Do you write to-do lists?			
2. Do you priortize your to-do lists according to what items have the highest pay-off for you?			
3. Do you complete all of the items on your to-do lists?			
4. Do you update your short-term and long-term goals regularly?			
5. Is your work area clean and organized?			
6. Do you put everything in its place?			
7. Do you deal effectively with interruptions?			
8. Can you easily find items in your work area?			
9. Do you focus on preventive problems?			
10. Do you make the best use of your time?			
11. Do you meet deadlines with time to spare?			
12. Are you on time to work, meetings, and events?			
13. Do you delegate well?			
14. When you are interrupted can you return to work without losing momentum?			
15. Do you do something everyday that moves you closer to your long-range goals?			
16. Do you do your most important work during your peak energy hours?			
17. Do you begin and finish projects on time?			
18. Do you handle each piece of paperwork once?			
19. Do you do small jobs during short time gaps?			
20. Do you maintain your flexibility?			

Scoring for Tool:

Give yourself: 5 points for every "Often"

3 points for every "Sometimes"

1 point for every "Rarely"

Total your points and see where you fit in this scale:

100-75: You manage your time very well.

74-50: You manage your time well most of the time, but need to be more consistent with your use of time-saving strategies.

49-25: You need to apply time management techniques.

24-0: You are overwhelmed, frustrated, and most likely under much stress.

Support Staff

**Time Management
Coaching Tool** (form continued)

Name: _____

Dept/School: _____

Date: _____

Keep a log of how you spend your time

Time	Activity
8:00 AM	
9:00 AM	
10:00 AM	
11:00 AM	
12:00 Noon	
1:00 PM	
2:00 PM	
3:00 PM	
4:00 PM	

Support Staff

Time Management
Coaching Tool (form continued)

Name: _____

Dept/School: _____

Date: _____

Analyze your own time management skills

Time	What goals were achieved?	What interruptions occurred?
8:00 AM		
9:00 AM		
10:00 AM		
11:00 AM		
12:00 Noon		
1:00 PM		
2:00 PM		
3:00 PM		
4:00 PM		

1. Identify the behavior(s) that you want to change or eliminate.
2. Define the new behavior(s) that you want to develop.
3. List the steps you will take to correct the bad behavior(s).
4. List the activities you will take to reinforce your new behavior(s).
5. Identify the people in your life who can help you support your new time management skills.

Support Staff

Time Management
Coaching Tool (form continued)

Name: _____

Dept/School: _____

Date: _____

REMEMBER: There are two types of work: ESSENTIAL and PRESSING

- *Essential work:* Work that contributes to your goals. They have long-term consequences.
- *Pressing work:* Work that has short-term consequences. It must be done NOW. It may or may not contribute to your long-range goals.

Desired prioritization of work:

Do First: Work that is ESSENTIAL & PRESSING
Do Second: Work that is ESSENTIAL but NOT PRESSING
Do Third: Work that is NOT ESSENTIAL but PRESSING
Do Last
(if at all):   Work that is NOT ESSENTIAL & NOT PRESSING

Essential and pressing	
Essential but not pressing	
Not essential but pressing	
Not essential and not pressing	

Support Staff

Time Management
Coaching Tool (form continued)

Name: _____

Dept/School: _____

Date: _____

Think about your priorities!

- How do you determine what is important to you?
- 80-20 rule: 80% of the value comes from 20% of your activities (the Pareto principle).
- When approaching your to-do list, do the important activities first, not the easy ones.
- Don't let unimportant items stop you from doing the activities that will help you achieve your goals.
- Don't always respond to other people's requests at the expense of your own priorities. Learn to say no tactfully and firmly.

- *Write your long-range goals. Aim for what you really want, and remember that your goals should be specific, measurable, achievable, and realistic and have a deadline.*

  1.

  2.

  3.

  4.

- *Write down your short-term goals for what you want to do today.*

  1.

  2.

  3.

  4.

Support Staff

Time Management
Coaching Tool (form continued)

Name: _____

Dept/School: _____

Date: _____

HELPFUL SUGGESTIONS:

Ways to say "No!" and mean it!

- Use your schedule
- Tell them why
- Be honest, but firm
- Provide options
- Know why before saying "yes"
- Don't feel obligated

Ways to avoid procrastination

- Admit you are delaying action
- Consider the consequences
- Take small steps along the way
- Delegate whenever possible
- Give yourself pep talks
- Reward yourself
- Set deadlines to which you feel committed

Ways to protect your time

- Remember your priorities
- Keep planned visits short and on schedule
- Discourage drop-in visits
- Rearrange furniture to put yourself in a stronger physical position
- Don't automatically be available for telephone calls that are not of an urgent nature
- Turn off your cell phone
- Don't encourage interruptions
- Resist reading junk mail
- Set up a file system with your important everyday categories as labels for each file
- Handle paper once, and place important items in your file system
- Schedule time for what you WANT to get done!!!

Ways to change your time management

- Identify your bad habit
- Identify a support group or individual to help keep you focused
- Begin your new behavior
- Practice the new behavior long enough until it becomes established

REMEMBER: *"Besides the noble art of getting things done, there is the noble art of leaving things undone. The wisdom of life consists in eliminating the non-essentials."*

—Chinese Proverb

Support Staff

**Time Management
Coaching Tool** (form continued)

Name: _____

Dept/School: _____

Date: _____

GOAL SETTING

- Determine long-range goals. Aim for what you really want. Write them down.
- Be sure to set goals that are specific, doable, and measurable and that have time lines.
- Review your goals daily.
- Determine short-range goals each day.

DEADLINES

- Set deadlines and timelines for all projects and activities. Categorize them according to:
    Important and urgent
    Important but not urgent
    Urgent but not important
    Neither important nor urgent
- Start with the important things first, instead of the quick, easy, enjoyable things.
- Learn when to say no. Do it logically, firmly, and tactfully.

SCHEDULING

- Schedule the most important activities for each day.
- Prepare tomorrow's schedule before you leave work today.
- Make a list of small mini-jobs that require a few minutes. When you have time gaps, do one of the mini-jobs instead of wasting those minutes.

PAPERWORK

- Incoming paper should be handled only once.
- When handling paperwork, there are four options:
    Dump it. Delegate it. Do it. Delay it.

PROCRASTINATION

- Conquer procrastination by:
    Admitting that you are delaying action
    Considering the consequences if you continue to delay
    Taking small steps
    Delegating the task if possible
    Giving yourself a pep talk
    Rewarding yourself for completing a task
    Committing yourself to action by setting deadlines

Support Staff

Name: _____

Dept/School: _____

Date: _____

Individual Development
Plan for Time Management
Select 2–3 goals

Problem to be Improved	Strategies	Date to be Completed
1.		
2.		
3.		

TIME MANAGEMENT REFERENCES

Alexander, R. (1992). *Common sense time management.* New York: AMACOM.

Allsands.com (2001). *Get organized!* [Online] Available at http://www.allsands.com/Home/ tipsfettingorg ha gn.htm

Bridges.com. (2000). *Organizational skills.* [Online] Available at http://www.at.bridges. com/20020108/ skills/main.htm.

Covey, S. (1994). *First things first.* New York: Simon and Schuster.

Ferner, J. (1995). *Successful time management.* New York: John Wiley and Sons.

Fisher, K., & Fisher, M. (2001). *The distance manager.* New York: McGraw Hill.

Lakelin, A. (1989). *How to get control of your time and your life.* New York: Dutton.

Mackenzie, A. (1997). *The time trap.* New York: AMACOM.

McLaughlin-Hale, J. (1999). *Organizational skills.* [Online] Available at http://www. stretcher.com/stories/99/991018m.cfm

Morgenstern, J. (2000). *Time management from the inside out: The foolproof system for taking control of your schedule and your life.* New York: Henry Holt and Co.

The Container Store. (2000). *Five keys to an organized work space.* [Online] Available at http://www.containerstore.com/browse/tips/organizedWorkSpace.jhtml

Wetmore, D. (2000). *Maintaining daily balance.* [Online]. Available at http://www. onlineorganizing. com/Client Article Maintaining Daily Balance/htm

CONCLUSION

This chapter includes coaching tools for general interpersonal skill development. Employees in task-specific roles may perform their technical skills well, but if their interpersonal skills interfere with their workplace relationships, then they will not be successful in their jobs. School leaders should use these tools as a place to start and should also strongly encourage their staff members to use the reference lists at the end of each tool's section.

Chapter Five

Summative Performance Appraisals

After investing 6 to 12 months' coaching and mentoring time as well as material resources in your staff members, the summative performance appraisal meeting is the occasion where the employee's accountability must be evaluated. Up to this point the supervisor has held a number of private meetings with each teacher or support staff member to assess the job skills require (the specific job competencies) and the individual's ability levels in each of those areas. The areas for growth were identified, and the employee was assisted in the development and implementation of his or her improvement plan. It is now time to measure the results of everyone's efforts. This is the purpose of the performance appraisal meeting.

The following summative forms for both teachers and support staff are general and are not intended to take the place of a school district's current summative forms unless they are adopted by the district and its teacher and support staff associations. Yet they are excellent summative models, as they include all of the items for which self-appraisal forms and coaching tools in specific skill areas have been provided in the previous two chapters. In using these forms, remember to follow the steps outlined in Chapter 1 on how to conduct effective performance appraisal meetings:

- Open the meeting by posing broad opening questions to the employee regarding his or her own thoughts about his or her performance.
- Respond thoughtfully to his or her comments and then identify what you perceived to be his or her accomplishments and areas for improvements.
- Review the employee's success in implementing his or her professional development plan. Summarize the employee's strengths and improvement needs.

- Recycle the improvement plan. Help the employee revise an outline for growth for the next cycle. (This will not occur if the employee has not achieved an acceptable level of improvement and will have to be terminated.)
- Evaluate and rate the employee's performance.

Throughout this meeting the employee may become defensive. Use effective feedback techniques, rephrase your comments to help the employee better understand your thoughts, and be empathetic—but firm if necessary. Remember, each staff member affects the learning and well-being of the students for which you are responsible. *You are accountable to them!*

Summative Performance Appraisal Self-Assessment

Teachers

Name: _____

Dept/School: _____

Date: _____

Reflect on your teaching performance in all five areas. Complete the self-assessment by using the levels of performance listed below. Discuss your performance in all areas at the initial performance appraisal meeting. Ask for coaching assistance in any areas where you feel you would like some help.

Levels of Performance

3 = **Exceptional**
2 = **Effective**
1 = **Not Yet Met**

3 = **Exceptional**—The teacher demonstrates **considerable mastery** of the concepts underlying this component and implements it in a **superior manner**.

2 = **Effective**—The teacher **demonstrates an understanding** of the concept underlying the component and implements it **effectively**.

1= **Not Yet Met**—The teacher **does not yet demonstrate an understanding** of the concepts underlying the component. Student learning may be jeopardized.

Area 1: Building Community	
Creating a Caring Environment	
Demonstrating Enthusiasm	
Planning Procedures and Routines	
Developing Classroom Rules	
Maintaining Behavioral Standards	
Creating the Physical Environment	

Area 2: Designing Learning	
Displaying Content Knowledge and Practice	
Recognizing Individual Differences	
Articulating Instructional Goals	
Using Materials and Resources	
Designing Units and Lessons	
Assessing Learning	

Area 3: Managing Learning	
Communicating Verbally and Nonverbally	
Asking High-Quality Questions	
Facilitating Learning Experiences	
Giving Feedback	
Making Instructional Adjustments	

Area 4: Communicating	
Keeping Accurate Records	
Communicating With Families	
Serving and Advocating for Students	

Area 5: Growing Professionally	
Reflecting on Teaching	
Assuming Professional Leadership	
Developing Professionally	

I would like coaching in the following area(s): _____

_____

_____

Action Plan

Teachers

Name: _____

Dept/School: _____

Date: _____

1. Goal for performance improvement:

2. Coaching tool(s) given to teacher:

3. Date and time when coaching tool(s) will be completed and discussed:

   Date: _____

   Time: _____

4. Date and time for follow-up observation:

   Date: _____

   Time: _____

5. Status of goal for performance improvement.

Signatures:

Teacher: _____ Date: _____

Administrator: _____ Date: _____

Summative Performance Appraisal

Teachers

Name: _____

Dept/School: _____

Date: _____

Levels of Performance

3 = Exceptional
2 = Effective
1 = Not Yet Met

3 = Exceptional—The teacher demonstrates **considerable mastery** of the concepts underlying this component and implements it in a **superior manner**.

2 = Effective—The teacher **demonstrates an understanding** of the concept underlying the component and implements it **effectively**.

1= Not Yet Met—The teacher **does not yet demonstrate an understanding** of the concepts underlying the component. Student learning may be jeopardized.

Area 1: Building Community

_____   **Creating a Caring Environment**
The teacher will create a classroom environment where all members of the learning community demonstrate genuine, consistent care and respect for each other.

_____   **Demonstrating Enthusiasm**
The teacher will demonstrate enthusiasm for the content. Students reflect this attitude through active participation, curiosity, and attention to detail and by having pride in their work.

_____   **Planning Procedures and Routines**
The teacher will design procedures and routines that allow students to learn, be successful, and function effectively in the classroom. Procedures will be explained to students and students will be given opportunities to practice.

_____   **Developing Classroom Rules**
The teacher will develop classroom rules that are guidelines or benchmarks that assist students in examining their behavior.

_____   **Maintaining Behavioral Standards**
The teacher will make sure that conduct standards are clear to students and students exhibit appropriate behavior. The teacher's response to any misbehavior is appropriate, successful, and respectful of the students' dignity.

_____   **Creating the Physical Environment**
The teacher will arrange a classroom in ways that promote efficient learning and minimize behavioral problems.

Summative Performance Appraisal
Page 2 (form continued)

Teachers

Name: _____

Dept/School: _____

Date: _____

Area 2: Designing Learning

_____   **Displaying Content Knowledge and Practices**
The teacher will display extensive content knowledge and demonstrate a commitment to the continuing pursuit of such knowledge. This will include continually searching for best practices to teach content most effectively.

_____   **Recognizing Individual Differences**
The teacher will demonstrate a solid comprehension of student's varied learning profiles, ability or readiness levels, interests, and cultural heritage and will recognize what implications these have for instructional planning. The teacher will also display knowledge of the typical developmental characteristics of the students' age group.

_____   **Articulating Instructional Goals**
The teacher will clearly articulate how goals establish high expectations and relate to curriculum frameworks and standards. All goals are clear, written in the form of student learning, and can be accurately assessed.

_____   **Using Materials and Resources**
The teacher will take steps to utilize school and district materials and resources and will actively seek out additional resources that will be used to enhance instruction.

_____   **Designing Units and Lessons**
The teacher will create a series of learning activities within an instructional unit. This sequence will be logical and will engage students in meaningful learning activities.

_____   **Assessing Learning**
The teacher will develop an assessment plan that will include a variety of assessments. The assessments will address all of the instructional goals and reflect developmentally appropriate student participation.

Area 3: Managing Learning

_____   **Communicating Verbally and Nonverbally**
The teacher will use spoken and written language that is clear, correct, and expressive. Well-chosen vocabulary will be used when giving directions and explaining procedures to students.

Summative Performance Appraisal
Page 3 (form continued)

Teachers

Name: _____

Dept/School: _____

Date: _____

_____ **Asking High-Quality Questions**
The teacher will use skilled, uniformly high-quality questioning to engage students in an exploration of content. Students have adequate time to respond to questions. Students formulate their own high-quality questions.

_____ **Facilitating Learning Experiences**
The teacher will design learning experiences that will engage students with content. These learning experiences will challenge students to construct deep understandings.

_____ **Giving Feedback**
The teacher will provide students with regular, timely feedback on their performance to help students assess their progress.

_____ **Making Instructional Adjustments**
The teacher will make adjustments to a lesson if students are not learning successfully. The teacher will also enhance instruction based on students' questions or interests. The teacher is responsive to special needs students and draws upon a repertoire of strategies to meet the needs of these students.

Area 4: Communicating

_____ **Keeping Accurate Records**
The teacher will develop effective systems for maintaining information on student completion of assignments and for keeping track of student progress in learning. The teacher will also develop effective record keeping systems for noninstructional activities.

_____ **Communicating With Families**
The teacher will frequently communicate with parents or guardians about the instructional program. Information is communicated to parents or guardians on both positive and negative aspects of student progress and parental concerns are handled with sensitivity.

_____ **Serving and Advocating for Students**
The teacher will be highly proactive in serving and advocating for students. The teacher will also make sure that all school-related decisions are based on the highest professional standards.

Summative Performance Appraisal
Page 4 (form continued)

Teachers

Name: _____

Dept/School: _____

Date: _____

Area 5: Growing Professionally

_____   **Reflecting on Teaching**
The teacher will reflect on units and lessons by asking thoughtful questions and making accurate assessments of outcomes and then use this information to make improvements.

_____   **Assuming Professional Leadership**
The teacher will take initiative for assuming leadership in school and district projects. The teacher will also develop supportive and cooperative relationships with colleagues.

_____   **Developing Professionally**
The teacher seeks opportunities for professional development and initiates opportunities to make important contributions to the profession, such as mentoring new teachers or supervising student teachers, writing articles for publication, and making presentations.

Comments:

Signatures:

Teacher: _____ Date: _____

Administrator: _____ Date: _____

Support Staff

Summative Performance Appraisal Self-Assessment

Name: _____

Dept/School: _____

Date: _____

Reflect on your position performance in all areas. Complete the self-assessment by using the levels of performance listed below. Discuss your performance in all areas at the initial performance appraisal meeting. Ask for coaching assistance in any areas where you feel you would like some help.

Levels of Performance

3 = Exceptional
2 = Effective
1 = Not Yet Met

3 = Exceptional—The support staff member exceeds district standards with the concepts underlying this component and implements it in a **superior manner**.

2 = Effective—The support staff member **demonstrates an understanding** of the concept underlying the component and implements it **effectively**.

1= Not Yet Met—The support staff member **does not yet demonstrate an understanding** of the concepts underlying the component.

Area 1:	
Demonstrates knowledge of job.	
Demonstrates knowledge of equipment operation.	
Understands work strategies.	
Maintains records.	
Pursues professional growth and shares knowledge with others.	
Learns new skills and handles change readily.	

Area 2:	
Listening Skills	
Oral Communication Skills	
Conflict Communication Skills	
Nonverbal Communication Skills	
Conflict Management Skills	
Public Relations Skills	
Stress Management Skills	
Team Building Skills	
Time Management Skills	

I would like coaching in the following area(s):_____

_____

_____

Action Plan

Support Staff

Name: _____

Dept/School: _____

Date: _____

1. Goal for performance improvement:

2. Coaching tool(s) given to support staff member:

3. Date and time when coaching tool(s) will be completed and discussed:

Date: _____

Time: _____

4. Date and time for follow-up observation:

Date: _____

Time: _____

5. Status of goal for performance improvement:

Signatures:

Support Staff Member: _____ Date: _____

Administrator: _____ Date: _____

Support Staff

Summative Performance Appraisal

Name: _____

Dept/School: _____

Date: _____

Levels of Performance

3 = Exceptional
2 = Effective
1 = Not Yet Met

3 = Exceptional—The support staff member **exceeds district standards** with the concepts underlying this component and implements it in a **superior manner.**

2 = Effective—The support staff members **demonstrates an understanding** of the concepts underlying the component and implements it **effectively.**

1 = Not Yet Met—The support staff member **does not yet demonstrate an understanding** of the concepts underlying this component.

Area 1: Competencies Specific to Support Staff Member's Position

_____ **Demonstrates knowledge of job**
- Knowledge of regulations and guidelines
- Knowledge of district procedures

_____ **Demonstrates knowledge of equipment operation**

_____ **Understands and follows safe practices**

_____ **Demonstrates work strategies**
- Makes sound decisions based on the circumstances
- Maintains acceptable quality standards

_____ **Maintains records**
- Completion of required work
- Maintenance of records

_____ **Pursues professional growth and shares knowledge with others**

_____ **Learns new skills and handles change readily**

Summative Performance Appraisal
Page 2 (form continued)

Support Staff

Name: _____

Dept/School: _____

Date: _____

Area 2: Competencies Generic to All Support Staff Members' Positions

A. Communication Skills
Listening Skills

_____

- Listens to the ideas, feelings, and emotions expressed by co-workers, students, and other staff
- Lets the speaker finish before responding
- Paraphrases what the speaker said and gives feedback accurately
- When needing more information, asks for more explanation
- Sees situations from others' points of view

Oral Communication Skills

_____

- Plans communication with others to accomplish his or her goals
- Tries to speak in a positive manner
- Explains ideas clearly
- Attempts to not become frustrated when others do not share his or her opinions.
- Communicates tactfully, courteously, patiently, and effectively with students

Conflict Communication Skills

_____

- When attacked verbally, does not take it personally
- Tries to find nonthreatening ways to approach others about sensitive issues
- Is able to resolve problems without losing control of emotions
- When someone is hostile, tries to reflect his or her feelings; restates concerns; and resolves the problem
- Is able to receive negative feedback without getting defensive

Nonverbal Communication Skills

_____

- Understands that it's not only what is said but how it is said that is important in communication
- Consistently attempts to maintain eye contact with the person with whom he or she is speaking
- Tries to convey interest, concern, warmth, and credibility in nonverbal behavior
- Frequently nods head to reassure someone who is sharing an idea or confidence
- Is aware of body posture at all times

Support Staff

Summative Performance Appraisal
Page 3 (form continued)

Name: _____

Dept/School: _____

Date: _____

_____

B. Conflict Management Skills
- When confronted with an individual who is difficult, is able to take action to improve the situation
- Is able to put problem people in perspective and not let them control his or her behavior
- When confronted by a difficult person, he or she is able to focus on problem solving
- Is able to deal directly with the behavior and not the difficult person's personality
- Uses a variety of specific strategies that serve as coping skills with various types of difficult people

_____

C. Public Relations Skills
- Understands the meaning of the terms internal and external public relations.
- Listens with empathy for solutions to people's problems
- Seeks to exceed people's expectations
- When he or she is not directly responsible for a hostile person's problem, he or she apologizes on behalf of the school and tries to find a solution
- Establishes and maintains good rapport with all students and staff
- Is reliable, consistent, and fair with all students and staff members
- Knows the school, staff, and program well. If he or she is not able to provide answers to people's questions, is able to refer them to someone who can help
- Exhibits good judgment and initiative in emergency situations
- Helps students and staff respect themselves and their school facilities
- Participates in school improvement and crisis intervention teams and demonstrates his or her unique perspectives to students, staff, and parents alike

_____

D. Stress Management Skills
- Is able to handle several problems or tasks at once
- Is able to control his or her temper when criticized or provoked
- Rarely feels out of control or overwhelmed
- Is rarely irritable, cynical, or negative
- Is not experiencing burnout on the job

Support Staff

Summative Performance Appraisal
Page 4 (form continued)

Name: _____

Dept/School: _____

Date: _____

_____

E. Team Building Skills
- Works for the common good of the team in an organized, diligent, and reliable manner
- Responds to questions with professional courtesy, is open and honest, shares information with all team members, and builds trust within the team
- Provides positive support that contributes to the goals of the team in a direct or indirect manner
- Works in a collegial way to achieve outcomes that require teamwork and takes ownership for his or her job within the established team goals
- Supports the members of the team in a way that is never negative toward other team members
- Effectively solicits input from all team members and provides feedback from team members in writing or in person-to-person communications
- Cooperates and works well with supervisors, subordinates, coworkers, and external contacts, and shares leadership when appropriate
- Tries consistently to learn new skills to bring to the team
- Manages conflict to enhance team performance and turns conflict into opportunities to generate new ideas and to strengthen relationships
- Accepts and contributes to new situations and changes

_____

F. Time Management Skills
- Makes long- and short-term goals and updates them regularly
- Prioritizes daily to-do list to accomplish the most urgent and important goals
- Deals effectively with interruptions and does not lose momentum with his or her current activity
- Does most important work during peak energy hours
- Maintains flexibility to accommodate emergencies and other unexpected events

Support Staff

Summative Performance Appraisal
Page 5 (form continued)

Name: _____

Dept/School: _____

Date: _____

Comments:

Signatures:

Support Staff Member: _____ Date: _____

Administrator: _____ Date: _____

CONCLUSION

What if you did everything you could to coach and support an employee to improve his or her performance, but he or she did not succeed? You then need to review carefully your district's policies and consult with your district's legal representative, as well as review all of your documentation that you have collected over the review period. Your district undoubtedly has a policy for handling unsatisfactory employees. Follow it closely, and maintain the required timelines. One missed deadline can nullify a year's worth of work and documentation. *It is important to remember that a principal's goal is to develop his or her staff's capacity to help students learn and achieve.* However, one ineffective elementary school teacher can negatively impact 28 children, and one weak secondary school teacher can negatively influence 150 students! We cannot afford to sacrifice that many students. You must take the responsibility of reviewing your faculty's and staff's performance seriously!

Chapter Six

Conclusion

Effective assessment and evaluation are two of the critical components of effective schools. Yet the performance appraisal process, whether developed by the state as in Texas, California, or Kentucky or implemented with local assessment tools, is a function of school leadership that frequently takes a back seat to other educational tasks. The lack of attention to the role of evaluation remains an important variable in school improvement initiatives, as it is the very process of evaluation that should serve to drive decision making for the school. It is through the collection of baseline data for the individual employee that improvement can be measured and discussed, goals developed, and plans implemented.

The process of performance appraisal is critical for the administrator who is attempting to improve student performance, as it is during the conferencing with staff members that an opportunity is afforded to set the tone of expectations, to build a team, and to value and recognize those skills and attributes that lead to quality teaching and learning. Through this developmental approach individual mentoring can occur between the teacher and the administrator or the support staff member and the administrator, as the performance appraisal conference lends itself to focusing upon both the individual's performance and the performance within the larger group.

All school staff members must be held accountable to perform their responsibilities in ways that support student learning and student well-being. Administrators must be accountable to superintendents and school boards not only for their students' achievement, but also for their staff's growth and development. No one individual can make a difference by him or herself. It takes the efforts of everyone in the school community—including parents and the students themselves—to increase students' achievement levels.

**CORWIN
PRESS**

The Corwin Press logo—a raven striding across an open book—represents the union of courage and learning. Corwin Press is committed to improving education for all learners by publishing books and other professional development resources for those serving the field of K–12 education. By providing practical, hands-on materials, Corwin Press continues to carry out the promise of its motto: **"Helping Educators Do Their Work Better."**